Th
Stamford
Raffles

Thomas Stamford Raffles

Schemer or Reformer?

Syed Hussein Alatas

With an introduction by
Syed Farid Alatas

NUS PRESS
SINGAPORE

© 1971 Syed Hussein Alatas

© 2020 Syed Farid Alatas (introduction)

Published by:

NUS Press
National University of Singapore
AS3-01-02, 3 Arts Link
Singapore 117569

Fax: (65)6774-0652
Email: nusbooks@nus.edu.sg
Website: http://nuspress.nus.edu.sg

ISBN: 978-981-325-118-2

National Library Board, Singapore Cataloguing in Publication Data

Name(s): Alatas, Hussein, Syed, 1928-2007.
Title: Thomas Stamford Raffles : schemer or reformer? / Syed Hussein Alatas.
Description: Singapore : NUS Press, 2020. | "First published by Angus & Robertson
    (Publishers) Pty Ltd in 1971."--Title page verso. | Includes bibliographical
    references.
Identifier(s): OCN 1135729430 | ISBN 978-981-32-5118-2 (paperback)
Subject(s): LCSH: Raffles, Thomas Stamford, Sir, 1781-1826. | Colonial
    administrators--Singapore--Biography. | Colonial administrators--Indonesia--
    Biography. | Colonial administrators--Great Britain--Biography. | Singapore--
    History--20th century. | Indonesia--History--20th century.
Classification: DDC 959.5703092--dc23

First published by Angus & Robertson (Publishers) Pty Ltd in 1971.

Printed by: Markono Print Media Pte Ltd

Contents

Preface

My father, Syed Hussein Alatas, had been concerned with the problems of colonialism since his student days at the University of Amsterdam during the 1950s. In an article he wrote for the periodical *Eastern World* (November 1956), entitled "Some Fundamental Problems of Colonialism", he suggested that the greatest damage caused by colonialism was in the sociological, psychological and cultural areas of life. This is because these problems hampered solutions in other fields. Colonialism created a group among the intelligentsia whose orientation was largely Westernised. When this group took over the administration of the nation upon political independence, they had already been cut off, to some extent, from their own cultural heritage. Thus, they were unable to integrate tradition with modern Western thought. Added to that was the sense of inferiority that they had, owing to the long years of domination by the colonial power and the gradual "realisation" that their "weakness" and "backwardness" was inherent in their way of life.

Alatas' concern with the fundamental problems of colonialism later found expression in his seminal work, *The Myth of the Lazy Native: A Study of the Image of the Malays, Filipinos and Javanese from the 16th to the 20th Century and its Function in the Ideology of Colonial Capitalism*, published in 1977. This study attacks the colonial construction of the idea of the lazy native, explaining how it is grounded in the interests of the British colonisers that were tied to capitalism in the colonies. The problem, however, was that this idea of inherent native incapacities became internalised by the native intellectuals themselves and was even promoted by them well into the post-colonial period. The point is that colonial rule resulted in the colonised coming to see themselves in the way that the colonisers saw them. The colonised also viewed the colonisers as superior to themselves and this feeling continued after independence.

This, indeed, may partly explain the adulation of Raffles, the "founder" of Singapore. Years before publishing *The Myth*, my father wrote the present work, *Thomas Stamford Raffles: Schemer or Reformer?*, first published in 1971, four years after he took up the position of Professor and Head of the Department of Malay Studies at the University of Singapore. The book was dedicated to me. I had not yet reached my teenage years but was old enough to be thrilled at having my name printed on a page in a book. I was not surprised by the general attitude of the book as I had heard much of my father's views on Raffles during dinner time conversations at home.

Therefore, I was quite surprised when a *Straits Times* reader made some negative remarks about my father's views on Raffles in 1979. The reader had written a letter to *The Straits Times* ("Raffles not against Chinese and Malays", 20 June 1979) as a response to the views my father had expressed on Raffles at a forum on "The Relevance of Traditional Values in Singapore". At the forum he stated that Raffles was an unscrupulous administrator and was biased against the Chinese and Malays ("Professor: Raffles was glorified", *The Straits Times* 7 June 1979). The reader who responded took a rather uncritical stance toward the coloniser. By that time, I was an A level student and took it upon myself to reply, stating that there was evidence of Raffles' prejudiced views and misdeeds ("That doesn't cancel out the reality of his prejudices...", *The Straits Times* 3 August 1979).

I remember feeling very proud that my letter to the Forum section of *The Straits Times* appeared in print, as proud as I am now to be able to present this new edition of my father's *Thomas Stamford Raffles: Schemer or Reformer?*

Syed Farid Alatas

Introduction

Must Raffles Fall?[1]

In a letter to Colonel Addenbrooke, dated 10 June 1819, Thomas Stamford Raffles wrote that on Singapura he had "just planted the British flag" which was to be a "more commanding and promising Station for the protection and improvement of all our interests in this quarter…".[2] The year 2019 marked the 200th anniversary of the arrival of Thomas Stamford Raffles in Singapore. In this book, *Thomas Stamford Raffles: Schemer or Reformer?*, first published in 1971, Syed Hussein Alatas argues for a more critical appraisal of Raffles. As Singapore commemorated the 200th anniversary of British colonial "found-

1. I would like to thank Amy Soh Geok Peng for assisting me in the preparation of this introduction.
2. W. W. Williams & T. S. Raffles, "The Founding of Singapore", *Journal of the Malaysian Branch of the Royal Asiatic Society* 42, 1(1969): 71–7, p. 71.

ing" of Singapore with a national bicentennial in 2019, this new edition of Alatas' book is appropriate in order to contribute to the discussion on the man as a colonial agent and the broader meaning of colonialism.

In most countries, the idea of nominating an imperialist as the founder of a newly independent state would have been considered "outrageous and most definitely reactionary".[3] But, when *Thomas Stamford Raffles* appeared in 1971, the dominant view in Singapore was that it was inadvisable to search for a "golden past" in the pre-colonial era as history prior to 1819 was one of "ancestral ghosts" and should be forgotten.[4] K. G. Tregonning (1923–2015), formerly Raffles Professor of History at the University of Singapore, had this to say: "Modern Singapore began in 1819. Nothing that occurred on the island prior to this has particular relevance to an understanding of the contemporary scene; it is of antiquarian interest only."[5]

Thus, history began after 1819 and Raffles, as the prime mover, was elevated to a "Great Man" of history, not only by colonial historians, but also officially by the post-

---

3. "Raja Tells Why We Still Honour Raffles' Name", *The Straits Times*, 25 May 1983.
4. S. Rajaratnam, "Untitled Speech", in Chan Heng Chee & Obaid Ul Haq, eds., *The Prophetic and the Political: Selected Speeches and Writings of S. Rajaratnam*, Singapore, Graham Brash, 1987, p. 140; S. Rajaratnam, "S'pore's Future Depends on Shared Memories, Collective Amnesia", *The Straits Times* 20 June 1990.
5. K. G. Tregonning, "The Historical Background", in Ooi Jin-Bee & Chiang Hai Ding, eds., *Modern Singapore*, Singapore: Singapore University Press, 1969), p. 14.

colonial state.[6] It was stressed that history after 1819 was something that all Singaporeans could identify with because of the collective memories that Singaporeans of all races had and shared. The mistake would be to regress into the past. The then Foreign Minister, S. Rajaratnam, said that "[t]he more we were inspired by our past, the greater our awareness of our differences and separateness and the greater the chances of a multiracial society collapsing through racial fears and violence."[7] In another speech on the occasion of the celebration of the founding of Raffles Institution, Rajaratnam acknowledged the strangeness of such a ceremony as the one he was presiding over and proceeded to answer the question as to why Singapore elected to nominate an imperialist as the founder of the now independent state?[8] Rajaratnam's answer was that this was recognition of the facts that Raffles founded Singapore as a free port, and had a vision for its future as a great trading centre. Had this not happened, the ancestors of Singaporeans would have remained in China, India, Sri Lanka and Indonesia, and their descendants would be living a hard life in those countries trying to make ends meet.[9]

The coloniality of such a perspective is all the more

6. Kwa Chong Guan, "Introduction", in Kwa Chong Guan & Peter Borschberg, eds., *Studying Singapore Before 1800*, Singapore: NUS Press, 2018, pp. 1–26, pp. 3–4.
7. S. Rajaratnam, "National Values of Singapore", Seminar for Pre-university Students, 17–22 June 1974, Ministry of Education, Singapore.
8. "Raja Tells Why We Still Honour Raffles' Name".
9. "Raja Tells Why We Still Honour Raffles' Name".

glaring when we take into consideration the growing critical literature on colonialism in the form of post-colonial theory and decolonial thought.

Scholarship on Singapore's history has progressed since 1971. No longer is Singapore history said to have begun in 1819. It is now known that it began 500 years before that in 1299 as the seaport of Temasek.[10] The authors of *Singapore: A 700-Year History* state that their book differs from other works on the history of Singapore by providing a long-sighted view of the past, dating the start of Singapore's history with the arrival of Sri Tri Buana from Palembang, about 500 years before Raffles arrived here.[11]

What has not changed, however, is Raffles' position as a "Great Man" of history. In post-colonial Singapore, Raffles is to this day a canonised figure. Boulger laments that Raffles was "unlucky in [that] his achievements were far from recognised in his own lifetime".[12] This was to be overcompensated for in post-colonial Singapore where his name lives on in a variety of forms. First and foremost are the two statues. The first is a 19th-century bronze statue that now stands in front of the Victoria Theatre and Concert Hall. The second was cast in polymarble in the 1970s, and can be found on the south bank of the

10. https://www.bicentennial.sg/about/.
11. Kwa Chong Guan, Tan Tai Yong & Derek Heng, *Singapore: A 700-Year History – From Early Emporium to World City*, Singapore: National Archives, 2009. See also the important work, Kwa Chong Guan & Peter Borschberg, eds., *Studying Singapore Before 1800*.
12. Demetrius Charles Boulger, *Life of Sir Stamford Raffles*, London: Charles Knight, 1973, p. xi.

Singapore River. Several landmark buildings, businesses, highly ranked educational institutions, prestigious clubs, and transport facilities have been named after Raffles. The world's largest flower, the *Rafflesia*, a genus of parasitic flowering plants, is also named after him.

How is it that a British colonial administrator would eventually attain a glorified, heroic status as a humanitarian reformer? While it is quite understandable that this would be the case with his British biographers, it is surprising that the post-colonial state of Singapore had adopted a very positive image of the man.[13] In fact, Raffles had been presented by the independent Singapore state as a hero of sorts, one of the rare instances in history of a colonial administrator serving as a national icon, in a world where most post-colonial nations adopt an extremely critical approach towards colonialism and the colonial figures who ruled over them.[14]

An interesting example comes from Rhodes Must Fall, a post-apartheid protest movement that was originally directed against a statue of Cecil John Rhodes, the British

13. The decision to keep the statue was based on the advice of the Dutch economic adviser to Singapore, Albert Winsemius, to Lee Kuan Yew. Winsemius' point was that keeping the statue was a friendly gesture to foreigners and signified that their capital would be safe in Singapore. See Lee Kuan Yew, *From Third World to First: The Singapore Story, 1965–2000*, New York: HarperCollins, 2000, p. 50.
14. An alternative account in literary form of the "founding" of Singapore can be found in the work of the Singaporean writer, Isa Kamari. See his novel, *Duka Tuan Bertakhta (Sadly You Rule)*, Kuala Lumpur: Al-Ameen Serve Holdings, 2011. For the English translation see *1819*, R. Krishnan, trans., Kuala Lumpur: Silverfish, 2013. See also Harry Aveling, "1819: Isa Kamari on the Foundation of Singapore", *Asiatic* 8, 2(2014): 88–108.

mining magnate and coloniser of Africa, located at the upper campus of the University of Cape Town (UCT), Africa's highest-ranking university. The bronze statue was made by the British figurative sculptor Marion Walgate and unveiled in 1934.[15] On 9 March 2015, a UCT student, Chumani Maxwele, flung faeces at the statue.[16]

So significant was the movement, defined by the slogan #RhodesMustFall, that the campaign for the statue's removal led to a wider movement to decolonise education across South Africa and received attention around the world. Calls for the removal of the statue had been heard decades ago. Afrikaner students had first demanded the statue's removal in the 1950s.[17]

During the first quarter of 2015, the Rhodes Must Fall movement dominated discussions at UCT. Finally, on 9 April 2015, after a prolonged student protest and a UCT Council vote the previous night, the statue was pulled down from its plinth at the University of Cape Town. This movement, however, was not merely about a decades-old statue. It has to be seen in the context of the

15. Jeremy Harding, "Rhodes Must Fall", *London Review of Books Blog*, 1 April 2015, https://www.lrb.co.uk/blog/2015/april/rhodes-must-fall, accessed 5 October 2019.
16. A. Verbaan, "UCT student in poo protest", *Cape Times*, 2015. http://www.iol.co.za/capetimes/uct-student-in-poo-protest-1829512, accessed 10 August 2019.
17. Sipho Masondo, "Rhodes: As divisive in death as in life", *News24*, 22 March 2015, https://www.news24.com/SouthAfrica/News/Cecil-John-Rhodes-As-divisive-in-death-as-in-life-20150322, accessed 20 January 2016.

continuing critique of the legacies of apartheid and the related question of the decolonisation of education.[18]

To most South Africans, Cecil Rhodes personified imperialism and racism. One of imperialism's strongest advocates, he had said:

> The object of which I intend to devote my life is the defence and extension of the British Empire. I think that object a worthy one because the British Empire stands for the protection of all the inhabitants of a country in life, liberty, property, fair play and happiness and it is the greatest platform the world has ever seen for these purposes and for human enjoyment.[19]

Colonial administrators and imperialists like Rhodes and Raffles should make us think about the meaning of colonialism. Colonialism was not only about political-economic domination and control. Colonialism did not only take the political-economic destiny of whole peoples out of their own hands but was also responsible for both the physical and epistemic destruction of peoples. In some cases, colonisation resulted in genocide and slavery. In other cases where colonialism took on a more "benign" form, it did constitute a kind of epistemicide.

In the *Manifesto of the Communist Party*, Marx and

---

18. For more on the movement, see Roseanne Chantiluke, Brian Kwoba & Athinangamso Nkopo, eds. *Rhodes Must Fall: The Struggle to Decolonise the Racist Heart of Empire*, London: Zed Books, 2018.
19. Robert I. Rotberg, *The Founder: Cecil Rhodes and the Pursuit of Power*, New York & Oxford: Oxford University Press, 1988, p. 103.

Engels noted that the bourgeoisie wanted to create a world after its own image:

> The bourgeoisie, by the rapid improvement of all instruments of production, by the immensely facilitated means of communication, draws all, even the most barbarian, nations into civilisation. The cheap prices of commodities are the heavy artillery with which it batters down all Chinese walls, with which it forces the barbarians' intensely obstinate hatred of foreigners to capitulate. It compels all nations, on pain of extinction, to adopt the bourgeois mode of production; it compels them to introduce what it calls civilisation into their midst, i.e., to become bourgeois themselves. In one word, it creates a world after its own image.[20]

People then came to view the world in line with that of the bourgeoisie, thereby providing ideological support for political-economic imperialism and capitalism. Part of that ideological justification for capitalism lay in cultural production, including the social sciences and humanities. In order for this to happen, there had to be the dismantling of the local and indigenous knowledge systems of the various societies that were to eventually be overrun by colonialism and capitalism. This took place through the process of what Santos and Grosfoguel refer to as "epistemicide" or the murder of knowledge, that is, the destruction of non-Western knowledge systems and dis-

---

20. Karl Marx and Frederick Engels, *Manifesto of the Communist Party*, Peking: Foreign Languages Press, 1963, p. 38.

courses.[21] In his elaboration of this concept, Grosfoguel discusses how several historical incidences of epistemicide functioned to erase local and indigenous knowledge, thereby contributing to the creation among the natives of a world view that was more in line with the interests of colonial capitalism. This epistemicide refers to the destruction of knowledge systems that were dominant in Asia, Africa and Latin America prior to capitalist and colonial expansion.[22]

Grosfoguel argues that there are four epistemicides of the modern period that created the socio-historical conditions that allowed for the possibility of the emergence of the epistemic racism and sexism that dominates the social sciences today. These four epistemicides are: i) the inquisition against Muslims and Jews after the conquest of Andalusia; ii) the genocides against indigenous peoples in the Americas and in Asia; iii) against African people in the context of transatlantic slavery; and iv) against women in Europe whose possession of certain forms of knowledge resulted in their being accused of witchcraft and burned alive for this crime.[23] There are other historical cases of epistemicide, many of which took place during the peri-

---

21. Boaventura de Sousa Santos, *Epistemologies of the South: Justice against Epistemicide*, Oxford: Routledge, 2014, pp. 92, 153; Ramon Grosfoguel, "The Structure of Knowledge in Westernized Universities: Epistemic Racism/Sexism and the Four Genocides/Epistemicides of the Long 16th Century", *Human Architecture: Journal of the Sociology of Self-Knowledge* 11, 1(2013): 73–90. http://www.okcir.com/Articles XI 1/Grosfoguel.pdf.
22. Grosfoguel, "The Structure of Knowledge in Westernized Universities".
23. Grosfoguel, "The Structure of Knowledge in Westernized Universities", 77.

ods of colonisation undergone by the majority of the peoples of Asia, Africa and Latin America. Epistemicide was crucial to the Eurocentric project of colonisation and the spread of capitalism because it resulted in the "natives" being unable to define and defend themselves, thereby being written off and condemned as mere objects of history.

It can be said, therefore, that there was no such thing as benign colonialism. Of course, it must be recognised, as noted by Rajaratnam, that the rule of Raffles as an imperialist in Singapore was not "marked by terror and savagery".[24] But, colonialism was always violent, often in a physical way, but always in a non-physical sense. The difference between various historical cases of colonialism was the impact on the colonised. In some cases, colonisation led to revolution. But in all cases, colonisation was founded not only on political-economic imperialism but also on epistemicide. One of the devastating effects of colonialism, and in fact, a direct consequence of epistemicide, is racism.

The British image of the native was founded on colonial racism. Various deficiencies and incapacities associated with the natives were explained in racist terms. Alatas noted that while capitalism in the home countries of Europe undermined and eventually destroyed the feudal system, in the colonies, colonial capitalism actually

24. "Raja Tells Why We Still Honour Raffles' Name", *The Straits Times*, 25 May 1983.

functioned to preserve the feudal order, with an underlying racist base. In other words, aspects of the old feudal system were perpetuated with a racial status system superimposed on it.[25] British colonial officers such as Raffles and John Crawfurd regarded the Malays as being rude and uncivilised in character, of feeble intellect, and at a low stage of intellectual development, indolent, submissive, and prone to piracy. Furthermore, the backwardness of the natives and their various negative traits were blamed on their religion, Islam.[26] Alatas emphasised that it was not just the petty officials, small traders, adventurers and politicians, but the best representatives of European civilisation that were responsible for colonial racism.[27] On the internalization of such views by the natives, Alatas says:

> In discussing the image which the indigenous people had of themselves we must bear in mind that some 20th century converts to this aspect of the colonial ideology are present among the indigenous people. An ideology is never confined to its originating group. It is also shared by those who are dominated by the system of which the ideology is the rationalization. During the time when slavery was current there were many slaves who believed in it. They shared the false consciousness inherent in the ideology.[28]

25. Alatas, *The Myth of the Lazy Native*, pp.18.
26. Alatas, *The Myth of the Lazy Native*, pp. 38–41.
27. Frantz Fanon, *Black Skin, White Masks*, trans. Charles Lam Markman, New York: Grove Press, 1967, pp. 90–1.
28. Alatas, *The Myth of the Lazy Native*, p. 132.

For Alatas, the lasting and devastating legacy of colonialism in the Malay world is the internalisation of the British image of the native by the natives themselves. The concomitant development of an inferiority complex among them is a serious consequence of colonial rule and a defining feature of the post-colonial society and politics.

In the post-colonial period, this auto-racism is the condition of coloniality without colonialism. As Fanon stated, there is only one destiny for the black man. He wants to be like the white man. He has long admitted "the unarguable superiority of the white man, and all his efforts are aimed at achieving a white existence."[29]

Alatas' *Thomas Stamford Raffles: Schemer or Reformer?* is an example of what Edward Said referred to as "revisionist" scholarship, that is, works that "set themselves the revisionist, critical task of dealing frontally with the metropolitan culture, using the techniques, discourses, and weapons of scholarship and criticism once reserved exclusively for the European."[30] Two examples of Syed Hussein Alatas' works that come under this category are *Thomas Stamford Raffles* and *The Myth of the Lazy Native*. In the latter work, Alatas exposes and critiques the ideological function of the colonial view of native indolence in colonial Southeast Asia, and the continuity of this ideology among the native elite themselves.

29. Fanon, *Black Skin, White Masks*, pp. 11, 63, 228.
30. Edward Said, *Culture and Imperialism*, New York: Vintage, 1993, p. 293.

In *Thomas Stamford Raffles*, Alatas presents a critique of the philosophy of Raffles at a time when there was hardly any critical assessment of the man in Singapore scholarship. Alatas' task was to present a critical and balanced, not Eurocentric or Anglocentric account of the thought and deeds of Raffles. His specific objective was to assess Raffles' political philosophy and conduct. Alatas felt that the silence among scholars about Raffles' questionable political philosophy and disturbing conduct was strange in that, even by colonial standards, he fell short of the humanitarianism that was attributed to him.[31]

Alatas had noted the ethnic bias of British historians and biographers in their treatment of Raffles. In their bid to present Raffles as a progressive statesman and humanitarian reformer, there is a virtual absence of critical treatment of Raffles' ethnically prejudiced views of the different Asian communities, his involvement in the Massacre of Palembang, the corruption case known as the Banjarmasin Affair, and other questionable acts, all of which should be put in the proper context of British imperialism and the ideology of colonial capitalism.

With respect to the Massacre of Palembang, Alatas leans towards the view that Raffles was complicit in the events that led up to the murders of twenty-four Europeans and sixty-three Javanese at the Dutch fort in Palem-

---

31. Syed Hussein Alatas, *Thomas Stamford Raffles: Schemer or Reformer?*, Sydney: Angus & Robertson, 1971, pp. 50–51.

bang, comprising soldiers and civilians.[32] On the Banjarmasin Affair or Banjarmasin Enormity, Alatas suggests that Raffles engaged in the suspicious acquisition of a territory along the Borneo coast by his friend, Alexander Hare, which involved nepotism and corruption.[33] Raffles had appointed Hare as Commissioner and Resident of Banjarmasin. The provision of labour supply to Hare included the transportation of forced labour from Java,[34] which in today's terms would amount to kidnapping, enslavement and human trafficking.[35]

During his lieutenant-governorship in Java as well as his time in Singapore, it is true that Raffles attempted to limit slavery by placing some restrictions on the local slave trade, keeping in line with British policy. Nevertheless, his biographer, Emily Hahn, claimed that Raffles himself kept a large retinue of slaves at his official residences in Java.[36] In other cases, Raffles had advocated for the replacement of slavery with contract labour and debt bondage.[37]

32. Alatas, *Thomas Stamford Raffles*, p. 18. For another view, according to which Raffles is held to have instigated the massacre, see Ahmat Adam, *Letters of Sincerity: The Raffles Collection of Malay Letter (1780–1824), A Descriptive Account with Notes and Translation*, Kuala Lumpur: Malaysian Branch of the Royal Asiatic Society, 2009.
33. Alatas, *Thomas Stamford Raffles*, pp. 34–5.
34. Alatas, *Thomas Stamford Raffles*, pp. 36–7.
35. Leon Moosavi, "Decolonising Criminology: Syed Hussein Alatas on Crimes of the Powerful", *Critical Criminology*, 2018. https://doi.org/10.1007/s10612-018-9396-9.
36. Emily Hahn, *Raffles of Singapore: a Biography*, Kuala Lumpur: University of Malaya Press, 1968, p. 290.
37. Alatas, *Thomas Stamford Raffles*, pp. 41, 47.

During the brief period of British rule over Java, Raffles was appointed Lieutenant Governor of Java (1811–1816). It was during this tenure that he was directly involved in the terrible events of 21 June 1812, the rape of Yogyakarta,[38] the cultural capital of Java, that ended in the killing of hundreds, and its looting and sacking.[39] Said to have been the first time an indigenous court was captured in this manner by a European army, the Yogyakarta *kraton* was stormed, damaged and looted by the British, with much of the contents of its archive stolen by Raffles.[40]

Raffles had also supported the opium trade and was concerned about how licensing would affect the East India Company's revenues. Viewing Singapore's function as an outlet for the distribution of opium throughout the region, he made every effort such that the Company's opium trade be "protected and offered every facility".[41]

38. Peter Carey, *The Power of Prophecy: Prince Dipanagara and the End of an Old Order in Java, 1785–1855*, Leiden: Brill, 2007. See chapter 7 entitled "The End of the Beginning: The Last Months of the Franco-Dutch Government and the British Rape of Yogyakarta", 1811–1812, pp. 261–343.
39. The barbaric nature of the attack on Yogyakarta was conveniently left out by Raffles himself in his *The History of Java*, 2 vols., London: Printed for Black, Parbury, and Allen, Booksellers to the Hon. East-India Company and John Murray, 1817. Of relevance to this discussion is Farish Noor, "Don't Mention the Corpses: The Erasure of Violence in Colonial Writings on Southeast Asia", *Biblioasia*, 15, 2(2019). http://www.nlb.gov.sg/biblioasia/2019/08/30/dont-mention-the-corpses-the-erasure-of-violence-in-colonial-writings-on-southeast-asia/, accessed 6 October 2019.
40. M. C. Ricklefs, *A History of Modern Indonesia since c. 1200*, 4th ed., Houndmills: Palgrave Macmillan, 2008, pp. 137–8.
41. Raffles to Mackenzie, 20 December 1819, enclosed in Raffles to Dart, 28 December 1819, vol. 50, Sumatra Factory Records, East India Company, National University of Singapore; India Office Library and Records. Lon-

Eventually, opium licenses were introduced, that is, "a certain number of houses may be licensed for the sale of madat or prepared opium".[42] Raffles' instructions to Farquhar were that these licenses were to be auctioned and re-auctioned "every three months until further orders". In addition to that, Raffles took for himself a 5 per cent commission on each opium license.[43] On the trade, Raffles said:

> Opium is one of the most profitable articles of eastern commerce: as such it is considered by our merchants… it is impossible to oppose trading in the same. In this situation of affairs, therefore, we would rather advise that general leave be given to import opium at Malacca, and to allow the expectation from thence to Borneo and all the eastern parts *not* in the possession of the state.[44]

The British opium trade out of Singapore that Raffles

don: Recordak Microfilm Service. 1960. Monash University. Cited in Nadia Wright, "Farquhar and Raffles: The Untold Story", *Biblioasia* 14, 4(2019). http://www.nlb.gov.sg/biblioasia/2019/01/21/farquhar-raffles-the-untold-story/, accessed 5 October 2019.

42. Raffles to Travers, 20 March 1820, vol. 50, Sumatra Factory Records, East India Company, National University of Singapore; India Office Library and Records. London: Recordak Microfilm Service. 1960. Monash University. Cited in Nadia Wright, "Farquhar and Raffles: The Untold Story", *Biblioasia* 14, 4(2019). http://www.nlb.gov.sg/biblioasia/2019/01/21/farquhar-raffles-the-untold-story/, accessed 5 October 2019.

43. Jennings to Farquhar, 15 August 1820, L. 4, SSR; Accountant General's office, 8 March 1826, vol. 71, Java Factory Records, East India Company, London, Recordak Microfilm Services, 1956. Microfilm, Monash University. Cited in Nadia Wright, "Farquhar and Raffles: The Untold Story", *Biblioasia* 14, 4(2019). http://www.nlb.gov.sg/biblioasia/2019/01/21/farquhar-raffles-the-untold-story/, accessed 5 October 2019.

44. *The History of Java*, vol. 1, p. 104. Cited in Hans Derks, *History of the Opium Problem: The Assault on the East, Ca. 1600–1950*, Leiden: Brill, 2012, p. 290.

sanctioned constituted Singapore's single largest source of revenue from 1824 until 1910.[45] Opium was also a major source of revenue during Raffles' governorship of Java.[46] The hypocrisy was lost on Abdullah bin Abdul Kadir Munshi, the Malay writer who was also for a time Raffles' scribe and copyist. While Abdullah counselled the Malays against the evils of opium smoking and praised the reputable Europeans for avoiding it, he seemed blind to the reality that while the Europeans did not consume opium, they traded in it, and even offered it, as Raffles did, to Malay emissaries.[47]

Raffles' supporters and admirers, as noted by Alatas, have generally remained silent about his questionable views and activities. The purpose of *Thomas Stamford Raffles* is to call for a balanced approach that on the one hand recognises his role in the founding of Singapore as a trading settlement, and on the other provides an accurate assessment of his political philosophy and his conduct in Java and Singapore that does not shy away from exposing his faults and hypocrisy as well as his possible involvement in the crimes of the powerful.[48]

45. C. Trocki, *Singapore: Wealth, Power and the Culture of Control*, London: Routledge, 2006, p. 20. Cited in Nadia Wright, "Farquhar and Raffles: The Untold Story", *Biblioasia* 14, 4(2019). http://www.nlb.gov.sg/biblioasia/2019/01/21/farquhar-raffles-the-untold-story/, accessed 5 October 2019.
46. Derks, *History of the Opium Problem*, Appendix 4.
47. A. H. Hill, "The Hikayat Abdullah", Journal of the Malayan Branch of the Royal Asiatic Society 28, pt. 3 (1955), p. 80. Cited in Alatas, *The Myth of the Lazy Native*, pp. 138–9.
48. On colonial hypocrisy see Aimé Césaire, *Discourse on Colonialism*, New York & London: Monthly Review, 1972, p. 11.

In fact, Alatas' work on Raffles can be viewed as a discussion of criminology in the decolonial mode.[49] To the extent that criminology as a field is Eurocentric, its research agenda is such that many topics and themes of great relevance to the South are omitted. One such theme is colonisation. Mainstream criminology does not take into account the role of colonialism in the interplay between past and contemporary globalization, global inequality and insecurity.[50] There is a silencing that goes on in Northern theory for which the colonial and coloniality are often deemed irrelevant. Missing or omitted is empire and the role of European capitalism in state formation, and the development of ideas and institutions, often accompanied by violence and criminal behaviour of the colonial state, but also the ideological criminalisation of anti-colonial resistance.[51] Another tendency of mainstream criminology is to focus on "low level crime", "street crime", "everyday crime", or "crimes of the powerless", at the expense of "crimes of the powerful".[52] The study of Raffles is at one and the same time a study of the

49. See Moosavi's important contribution to this idea in his "Decolonising Criminology: Syed Hussein Alatas on Crimes of the Powerful."
50. Katja Franko Aas, "Visions of Global Control: Cosmopolitan Aspirations in a World of Friction". In M. Bosworth and C. Hoyle, eds., *What is Criminology?* Oxford: Oxford University Press, 2011; Katja Franko Aas, "'The Earth is One but the World is Not': Criminological Theory and its Geopolitical Divisions", *Theoretical Criminology* 16, 1(2012): 5–20, pp. 13–14.
51. Kerry Carrington, Russell Hogg & Maximo Sozzo, "Southern Criminology", *British Journal of Criminology* 56(2016): 1–20, p. 8.
52. Moosavi, "Decolonising Criminology".

crimes of the powerful as well as the criminality of the colonial state.

On that matter, we have already referred to Alatas' discussion in *Thomas Stamford Raffles* on the Massacre of Palembang and the Banjarmasin Affair, both of which involved the criminality of the colonial state, as well as the issues of slavery and the opium trade.

Kwa notes perceptively that the idea of 1819 as the beginning of Singapore's history presents three categories of historiographical problems. One is attributing to Raffles the foreknowledge of Singapore's strategic importance, resulting in his elevation to a "Great Man" of history and the subsequent focus on generations of "great men". History is explained through the impact of great men. The second category of problems is that it possibly aggravated Singapore's post-1965 identity crisis by depriving it of its origins as a fourteenth-century Malay state. The third category of problems is that it distorts our perspective on the role of the Malay sultans and their courts in Singapore, suggesting that they were not active subjects in their own history.[53] To this we may add a fourth category of problems, that is, our attitude towards colonialism.

---

53. Kwa Chong Guan, "From Temasek to Singapore: Locating a Global City-State in the Cycles of Melaka Straits History", in Kwa Chong Guan & Peter Borschberg, eds., *Studying Singapore Before 1800*, NUS Press, 2018, pp. 179-205, pp. 201-3.

Alatas was open about the ideological motives of his work:

> I believe in the primarily negative influence of colonialism. I believe in the need to unmask the colonial ideology, for its influence is still very strong. Colonial scholars have on the whole avoided the study of the negative aspects of colonialism; an attempt to correct this should not be considered automatically as a reversal of the coin. It is the facts adduced, the evidence marshalled, the themes introduced, the analyses accomplished, and the attitudes of the scholar which should finally decide whether the attempt is merely a reversal of the coin or a real extension and supplementation of existing knowledge.[54]

The critical anti-colonial spirit is not completely absent in Singapore, as can be seen from Singaporean poet, Suratman Markasan's poem, "Balada Seorang Lelaki di Depan Patung Raffles" (The Ballad of a Man Before the Statue of Raffles), a few lines of which are reproduced below:

> Raffles smiles rigidly
> the man who has lost his mind grumbles
> "I've said it a thousand times
> you deceived my grandparents totally
> you seized their properties until it's gone, greedily
> you gave it away to your friends, enemies
> do you hear, Raffles? Do you hear?
> I should have brought you to face justice

---

54. Alatas, *The Myth of the Lazy Native*, p. 9.

at the UN office in New York

but unfortunately the judge has no clout."[55]

Thomas Stamford Raffles was never taken seriously in Singapore and was hardly engaged with academically. Apart from a debate between Alatas and the historian, Ernest Chew,[56] the subject was not discussed.[57]

To note that Raffles was a product of his time and was informed by the dominant ideology of his age, that is,

---

55. Suratman Markasan, "Balada Seorang Lelaki di Depan Patung Raffles - The Ballad of a Man Before the Statue of Raffles," in *Suratman Markasan: Puisi-puisi Pilihan - Selected Poems of Suratman Markasan*, Singapore: NLB, 2014, pp. 18–29.
"Raffles tersenyum kaku
Lelaki hilang kepala menggerutu
"Telah kukatakan seribu kali
kau menipu datuk-nenekku hidup mati
kau rampas hartanya pupus-rakus
kau bagikan kepada kawan-lawan
kau dengar Raffles? Kau dengar?
Seharusnya kau kubawa ke muka pengadilan
di PBB kota New York
tapi sayang hakim tak punya gigi."
56. See the debate between Alatas and historian, Ernest Chew, "A Controversy on Raffles", *Suara University* 3, (1972): 49–61. Part of this debate first appeared in the *New Nation* over three weeks in July 1972. See also Ernest Chew, "Raffles Revisited: A Review & Reassessment of Sir Thomas Stamford Raffles (1781–1826)", http://www.postcolonialweb.org/singapore/history/chew/chew2.html, accessed 5 October 2019. Chew refers to Alatas as belonging to or influenced by 19th-century Dutch scholarship on Raffles, which bore hostile to him on account of his five-year Governorship of Java and taking of Singapore. This scholarship, like that of Alatas later, had highlighted Raffles alleged misdeeds and abuses of power. Alatas did not agree with this characterisation, stating that he took a position between that of the British admirers of Raffles and his hostile Dutch detractors. See "A Controversy on Raffles", p. 52.
57. Suriani Suratman notes that the attitude towards Raffles in the arts scene differs in that there is a more critical stance taken, particularly in the performing arts, and in the visual and performance arts. Conversation with Suriani Suratman, 4 November 2019.

imperialism, is to state the obvious. In our assessment of him today, though, that recognition cannot be an excuse to allow the embarrassing facts of the colonial adventure to disappear. It is hoped that the new edition of this work will result in more critical discussions in Singapore about Raffles as well as the larger question of the meaning of colonialism. The call is not for the physical removal of the Raffles statues from their plinths, but for their symbolic fall.

Syed Farid Alatas
Departments of Sociology & Malay Studies
National University of Singapore

Thomas Stamford Raffles

Schemer or Reformer?

TO MY SON FARID

1

The General Framework
of Raffles' Political Philosophy

No work on the political philosophy of Thomas Stamford Raffles has ever been published. Except for a number of biographies which tend to repeat a fund of common knowledge, publications about Raffles usually deal with his administrative policies and his views on political affairs. History has been aptly defined as "the study of the dead by the living". It has also been suggested that contemporary interest partly determines our selection of problems and our foci of analyses. My present interest in Raffles and his philosophy stems from the need to make as complete as possible the picture we have of the man. I am not treating the subject as would an historian of ideas or of political philosophy. Raffles was not a political theorist such as Aristotle, Plato, Hegel, Marx, or de Tocqueville, or even his British contemporaries, Adam Smith and Robert Owen.

My treatment of Raffles' political philosophy is designed to clarify certain aspects of his biography. It is part of an attempt to explain intelligibly his thought and action within their philosophical framework. Once this is accomplished, what at times appear as contradictions in his views and attitudes will resolve themselves into a consistent pattern.

It is paradoxical that historians can sometimes adopt the most unhistorical of approaches. Biographies of Raffles have frequently been guilty of this. They have failed to view the thought and action of a maker of history in the light of changing circumstances. They have ignored the development of Raffles' thought and his reactions to the problems which surrounded him.[1] In addition to this fault there is the strong ethnic bias of British historians and biographers in favour of Raffles; so much so that it looks almost like a conspiracy.[2] To counteract this bias of British historians and biographers in favour of Raffles the best source to refer to is Raffles' own writings and papers.

On October 9, 1820 Raffles wrote to Thomas Murdoch from Benkulu (Bencoolen). This letter serves as an excellent starting point for an examination of the man's political philosophy. In it he wrote:

(1) "There appear to be certain stages and gradations

through which society must run its course to civilization, and which can no more be overleaped or omitted, than men can arrive at maturity without passing through the gradations of infancy and youth. Independence is the characteristic of the savage state; but while men continue disinterested, and with little mutual dependence on each other, they can never become civilized."

(2) "The acquisition of power is necessary to unite them and to organize society, and it would perhaps be difficult to instance a nation which has risen from barbarism without having been subjected to despotic authority in some shape or other. The most rapid advances have probably been made, when great power has fallen into enlightened and able hands; in such circumstances nations become wealthy and powerful, refinement and knowledge are diffused, and the seeds of internal freedom are sown in due time, to rise and set limits to that power whenever it may engender abuse. Freedom thus founded on knowledge and a consideration of reciprocal rights, is the only species that deserves the name, and it would be folly to conceive the careless independence of the savage as deserving of equal respect. In order to render an uncivilized people capable of enjoying true liberty, they must first feel the weight of authority, and must become acquainted with the mutual relations of society."

(3) "Whether the power to which they bow be the despotism of force, or the despotism of superior intellect, it is a step in their progress which cannot be passed over.

Knowledge is power, and in the intercourse between enlightened and ignorant nations, the former must and will be the rulers. Instead, therefore, out of an affected respect for the customs of savages, of abstaining from all interference, and endeavouring to perpetuate the institutions of barbarism, ought it not rather to be our study to direct to the advancement and improvement of the people, that power and influence with which our situation and character necessarily invests us?"[3]

(4) The different nations of the earth were ordered by Raffles theoretically into different grades of civilization, morally and politically. "It is very certain that on the first discovery of what we term savage nations, philosophers went beyond all reason and truth in favour of uncivilized happiness; but it is no less certain, that of late years, the tide of prejudice has run equally strong in the opposite direction; and it is now the fashion to consider all who have not received the impression of European arms and laws, and the lights of Revelation, as devoid of every feeling and principle which can constitute happiness, or produce moral good. The truth, most probably, as is generally the case, lies between the two extremes, and there is, no doubt, much difference according to the circumstances under which the people may have been placed. We find, in some of the Islands of the South Seas, people who are habitually mischievous, given to thieving, lazy, and intractable; in others, we find the opposite qualities; and philosophers, speculating upon the first data that are

afforded, without full and general information, are led to error."[4]

This philosophy was based on the idea of progress and the survival of the fittest. Its key notions were current in the Europe of his times. They were the stock-in-trade of Western imperialism.

(5) In order to perform the civilizing mission as Raffles conceived it, the best form of government to impose upon the conquered territory was despotism. This is apparent from his views quoted above. But what nation should provide the despot? Raffles thought of the English nation whom he considered as the most worthy and most qualified to civilize the world. In his letter to Nightingall of May 5, 1814 (Buitenzorg), Raffles spoke of those eastern islands affected by petty wars, backwardness, and political anarchy. "I have ever felt that the redress of these evils was in a great measure in the power of the English Nation, that it was worthy of their general character; that there was no other nation that possessed the means in an equal degree, even if it possessed the inclination."[5] Obviously then, Raffles considered the English nation the most qualified to provide despots to civilize the world, and thought of himself as a suitable despot.

(6) Raffles claimed that he was very popular with the people of Sumatra.[6] He considered Sumatra should be conquered and colonized by the English and desired to be made despot for five years during which time he would develop the country for the benefit of the English and

the native population. "I would open a high road along the centre of the Island, from one end to the other, and the rivers should be my transverse pathways. I would assume supremacy without interfering with the just independence of other states. I would be the protector of the native states. I would, in fact, reestablish the ancient authority of Menangkabau, and be the great Mogul of the Island. I would without much expense, afford employment for twenty or thirty thousand English colonists, and I would soon give employment to as much British tonnage, and as many British seamen as are now engaged in the West India trade."

Such is then the framework of Raffles' political philosophy. It is a simple philosophy, uncritical of its own foundation and comfortably accommodative of all sorts of prejudice and political manipulation. Philosophically speaking Raffles was a layman, not a scholar, but nonetheless his political philosophy was related to his conduct in the East. His conception of progress as applied to the indigenous inhabitants of Malaysia and Indonesia was basically constituted of the following elements:

(a) England should be accepted as the ruling nation, or ally, depending on what were the interests of England as Raffles saw them. For Sumatra, or for certain parts of it, the best thing would be to be ruled by England. For the Celebes, at one time, the best thing was to be the ally of England.[8] For the Sultanate of Palembang the best thing would be to be the protectorate of England. In yet another form British control was achieved by manipulating the native power holder and ruling in his name.

(b) Agriculture should be developed to produce cash crops required by the European market. The British export trade should be developed. Western capitalism was to be imposed on the societies of Malaysia and Indonesia.

(c) The imposition of the British and Western concepts of property relation, the individual ownership of land, taxation in money instead of in kind, should be accepted. In short, the system of money economy, wage labour and agrarian capitalism would be imposed.

(d) Where it was deemed necessary acceptance of British law would be imposed.

(e) As part of the civilizing process the natives were asked to look favourably on the Protestant form of Christianity.[10] Raffles described the effort to promote the objects of the Bible Society as "cultivating the waste and barren soil of the native mind".[11] He suggested that the Dutch and the English should co-operate in spreading Christianity.

(f) The Asians should accept a subordinate status to the colonial personnel, mainly provide the labour force for British and Western capitalism. Raffles said of his plan for the establishment of European colonies in Sumatra: "The Chinese and natives would be manual labourers, as the negroes are in the West Indies."[12] British capital, British talent and British rule were to control and initiate the exploitation of the country. Raffles was interested in introducing sugar cultivation into Sumatra. Labour and other conditions were more favourable than in Jamaica. He was happy with low subsistence wages for the Sumatrans.[13]

The policies outlined above are some of the major constituent elements of Raffles' concept of progress for the Malay Peninsula and Indonesia. His entire previous career in the East had been dominated by this concept of progress and his dedication to British imperialist interests. In the light of his concept and his dedication we can explain and clarify the nature of his intrigues, his private dealings and his authoritarian ways which, at times, were in conflict even with the East India Company and the British Government. Taking into account his political philosophy, Raffles' different and seemingly contradictory stands resolve themselves into a consistent and tenaciously pursued policy of persuasion, coercion and aggression, conflict or peaceful co-existence, humanitarian action or oppression, all depending upon the central motivation: the advancement of British imperial interest and his own career, both permissible for him. For evidence to illustrate these facts we shall examine two well-known cases in which Raffles was involved: the Massacre of Palembang in 1811, and the Banjarmasin Affair of Alexander Hare.

2

The Massacre of Palembang

When Lord Minto appointed Raffles as the Agent to the Governor-General in the Malay States, an avant-courier to prepare the way for the British expedition under Lord Minto, on October 19, 1810, the stage was set for him to approach the Malay Sultans, seeking their assistance against the Dutch. It was during this period, before the fall of Java to the British on August 16, 1811, that Raffles sought contact with the Sultan of Palembang, Mahmud Badruddin. In his letters to the Sultan, Raffles urged him to rid the Sultanate of the Dutch and take the British as his true friends, and to sign a commercial treaty with the British. These letters from Raffles were brought to public attention by the Dutch Governor-General of Java, J. C. Baud, in a published paper in 1852,[1] after the letters had fallen into Dutch hands through an old friend of Badruddin in Batavia. In 1816, when the Dutch returned to Java, Badruddin sent the letters to Batavia in an attempt to implicate Raffles in the Massacre, and hoping that he would be restored to his throne by the Dutch. In this way he could place the responsibility for the Massacre on the British.

British writers on Raffles have either kept silent on the subject or dismissed the matter with a few sentences. The subject has been entirely avoided by John Bastin, in a book on Raffles, although it is highly relevant to his theme and his assessment of Raffles as a humanitarian and paternal autocrat;[2] this, although Bastin is probably the most serious and most intense scholar on Raffles, perhaps the only specialist on Raffles in the professional and academic sense of the word. Emily Hahn, a panegyrist of Raffles, not only avoided the subject of his possible implication in the Massacre of Palembang, but committed the gross error of confusing the time and muddling her data.

The Massacre was supposed to have taken place just after the British occupation of Java, about three weeks later, not two months. Hahn suggests that the Massacre was a reaction to Raffles' commission sent to Palembang in November, whereas the fact was that it was this commission that first suspected that a massacre of the previous Dutch Resident and others in the factory had taken place.[3]

It has been suggested that the Massacre of Palembang took place on September 14, 1811, approximately eighteen days after the Dutch surrendered to the British in Java, (August 26, 1811). Twenty-four Europeans and sixty-three Javanese in the Dutch fort of Palembang, comprising soldiers and civilians and including the Resident, through a deception, were led to a boat and then drowned in the river. The Dutch were told that they were going to be taken to Malacca, to be delivered to the British, and thereafter taken to Batavia, from where the British were ruling Java. The Dutch Resident apparently believed this to be a plausible story. Earlier in February 1811, Raffles had requested Captain D. Macdonald (then lieutenant) to arrange for the evacuation of the Dutch to Malacca, but Sultan Badruddin refused owing to the danger that his son, Pangeran Ratu, who was then on a mission to Batavia, might be seized by Marshal Daendels. Macdonald then left Palembang as Raffles had instructed him not to remain more than forty-eight hours in there, whatever was the outcome of his mission.[4]

Early in November 1811, the tragedy was not yet widely known in Batavia and on November 3, 1811, Raffles sent the first mission to receive the surrender of the Dutch factory, and to find out what happened to it. The mission was also to make a treaty with the Sultan of Palembang, something which Raffles had worked for persistently since his days in Malacca. On arrival in Palembang the members of the mission were placed in a well-provided house, received by the Sultan but were not allowed to move around freely. They were virtually under house arrest. After a few days they were sent back to their ship.[5] The mission returned to Batavia on December 11, 1811, after failing to accomplish its objectives. The Sultan of Palembang refused to accept Raffles' conditions for commerce and dependency with the British but insisted instead on his sovereignty and the independence of Palembang. The reason he gave was that he had secured his freedom from the Dutch before the British received the surrender of the Dutch possessions in Indonesia.[6]

At the end of April 1812 Major-General Gillespie was sent to Palembang with a punitive force. He defeated Badruddin, dethroned him, and enthroned the Sultan's brother, Ahmad Najamuddin. A treaty was signed and the island most coveted by Raffles, Banka, together with Billiton and other adjacent islands, fell into British hands. Gillespie's report to Raffles on this expedition was published in the *Java Government Gazette*, June 13, 1812. As we are interested in Raffles' relation to the Massacre of Palembang there is no need for us to go deeper into the intricacies of the events surrounding the three-cornered intrigues and diplomacy between the Dutch in Java, Raffles, and the two Sultans of Palembang who were alternately enthroned and dethroned by each party. Certain Dutch authorities in Java and the Netherlands held the view that Raffles was partly responsible for the Massacre of Palembang because of the nature of his agitation and persistent encouragement to Badruddin to drive away the Dutch from Palembang. In one of his letters from Malacca, Raffles had used words which could be construed as the direct encouragement to physically exterminate the Dutch.

With the exception of Bastin and Wurtzburg, British admirers and writers on Raffles have completely avoided the subject. Wurtzburg's attempt to defend Raffles was ill-equipped partly because he presumably did not know Dutch, and he definitely did not know Malay as apparent from his reliance on Windstedt for the translation of the controversial passage in Raffles' letter to Badruddin. In addition to this he took recourse to an attack on Baud's character which appeared to be both misplaced and irrelevant.[7] Wurtzburg's defence of Raffles and attack on Baud had been criticized by Coolhaas.[8] These two articles and one by Bastin are probably the only ones on the subject in English, but reference to the Massacre was made (in English) by another Dutch author, van Klaveren, who held that Raffles was largely responsible for the Massacre of the Dutch in Palembang in 1811.[9]

When Raffles reached Malacca on December 4, 1810, the task with which Lord Minto had commissioned him was to establish contact with the native states of Indonesia and to set them against the Dutch. He was also to collect statistical military information on the Dutch troops. On February 4, 1811, Raffles instructed Captain Macdonald to deliver letters in person and to contact his agent Tunku Radin Mohammed at the court of Palembang. He noted that some presents were to be delivered to the Sultan, Badruddin.[10] In his letter to Badruddin delivered by Macdonald in the Malay language, Raffles mentioned the present of four cases of rifles and ten cases of ammunition.[11] Previous to this Raffles had written several letters to Badruddin and Baud reproduced five letters in Malay. One was dated 17 Zulkaidah 1224 A.H., and another, (following the one Macdonald brought), was dated 11 Rabiul Akhir 1226 A.H. There was one more letter referred by Raffles before the one of 17 Zulkaidah 1224 A.H. Raffles had sent letters to Badruddin through his agents Tunku Radin Mohammed and Syed Abu Bakar. An earlier letter of Raffles was not known to Baud. However Raffles must have been sending letters to Badruddin over a period of more than a year. In some of the letters reproduced by Baud Raffles insisted that he should get a reply, but apparently Badruddin did not react accordingly.

However there was apparently a reply from Badruddin and it was in a further letter from Raffles (dated 8 Safar at Malacca, the year is not stated) that the controversial passage was found:

> Ini yang kedua, mesti sobat beta buang habiskan sekali-kali segala orang Belanda dan Residentnya dan segala orang yang dibawah hukum Belanda, mana yang dudok sekarang ini didalam negeri Palembang jangan kasi tinggal lagi.[25]

The literal and accurate English translation is:

This is the second, my friend must throw away, finish entirely all the Dutch people and their Resident and all those that were under their authority, those that now reside in Palembang. Do not allow them to stay.

The controversial phrase "buang habiskan sekali-kali" may be rendered in English into the following: (a) "expel and finish them off entirely", or (b) "evict and make an end of them". I cannot see how Windstedt, on whom Wurtzburg relied, could have translated "buang habiskan sekali-kali" as "evict". His translation is the following: "You must evict (buang) all the Dutch without exception and their Resident and all their dependents; do not let them live in Palembang."[13] Windstedt had omitted the word "habiskan" or had considered an adequate translation to be "without exception".

In traditional Malay, and even now, the phrase "buang negeri" means "banish" or "expel". The phrase "habiskan dia" or "habiskan nyawanya" means "kill him". The general meaning of "habis" is finish. The addition of the suffix "kan" means "to cause to be finished", "to make an end". It is an imperative expression. Whatever Raffles' true intention was, when he used this phrase, the fact remains that the expulsion and physical extermination of the Dutch and those under their authority in September 14, 1811, in Palembang, was the most accurate translation into action of the phrase "buang habiskan sekali–kali".

Wurtzburg's attempt to clear Raffles of any blame concerning the Massacre was ill-equipped because of his reliance on Windstedt's translation. In another instance this translation is entirely misleading. In one letter Raffles indicated the Governor–General's (at Bengal) desire to establish a friendship with the Malay rulers and expressed the following:

> maka ini beta ada banyak chinta sama sahabat beta, mahu menjadi sahabat yang baik dengan berseh hati, yang jangan dibelakang hari bersahabat sama lain orang. Maka itu orang Belanda apa guna sahabat beta betulkan kasi tinggal dalam negeri Palembang kerana orang Belanda ada banyak jahat, dia mahu bikin satu jalan yang jahat juga sama sahabat saha- bat beta. Sebab itu beta ada banyak susah hati dari sahabat beta tiada jadi sahabat sama Kompeni Inggeris dan kalau sahabat beta ada suka menjadi sahabat yang betul sama Kompeni Inggeris mesti sahabat beta tentukan sekali-kali, lagi minta balas surat ini dan surat yang dahulu dengan begitu lekas, lagi dengan segala bicharanya orang Belanda dengan sahabat beta, lagi beta minta satu orang wakil dari- pada sahabat beta biar datang kepada beta.[14]

Windstedt's translation of the above was:

> I am very fond of you and beg you to become my candid friend and not to be friendly hereafter with others. What is the use of letting the Dutch live in Palembang? They are very bad people and want to take a bad line with you. So I am very sorry you are not good friends with the English Company. If you want to be its friend, you must make up your mind and reply to this and my former letter and with

[sic] all the negotiations with you I ask you to send a repre-
sentative [wakil] to me.[15]

The literal and accurate translation is:

> Therefore I have much love for my friend and desire to
> become a good friend with a pure heart who in days to
> come will not be the friend of another. Hence why should
> my friend allow the Dutch to stay in Palembang since they
> are bad [jahat]. They want to do bad also towards my
> friend. Because of this I feel very sad that my friend does
> not become the friend of the English Company, and if my
> friend would like to become the real friend of the English
> Company, my friend must make the decision, and also reply
> quickly to this and the previous letter, and [let me know of]
> the talks my friend held with the Dutch, and one represen-
> tative from my friend should be sent to me.[16]

Confusion and misinterpretation occurs because in
Windstedt's translation it was Raffles who expected the
Sultan not to be the friend of another while in the text it
was Raffles who offered not to be the friend of another.
The persuasive entreaty of Raffles is lost in Windstedt's
translation and this error is quite serious. It was hazardous
for Wurtzburg to argue on the basis of sources for which
he had no direct understanding and thereby rely on what
appears to be an erroneous translation. Since understanding of the content of the letters is imperative to assess the
time sequence, and since this helps to solve further problems, Wurtzburg's attempt was doomed at the outset.[17]

Raffles' persistent persuasion and offer of loyal friendship, the tone of his letters to Badruddin, his patience for his evasive reaction, the context of events discussed in the letter, all these are relevant to interpret Badruddin's reaction to the phrase "buang habiskan sekali-kali" and to judge Raffles' responsibility in connection with the Massacre.

The first report on the Massacre was submitted by Tunku Radin Mohammed and Syed Abu Bakar,[18] Raffles' two agents mentioned earlier, whom Raffles ordered to inquire the fate of the Dutch factory at Palembang and Badruddin's attitude towards the British. They arrived at Minto on July 22, 1811, before the British occupied Batavia. They returned to Penang, their home, from Palembang on December 7, 1811. By order of Farquhar they proceeded to Malacca and there submitted their report to the Members of the Court of Justice on December 13, 1811. The first report of the Massacre reached the British in December 1811 and Raffles' reaction to this Massacre was the expedition under Gillespie in April 1812. Whether Raffles' reaction to the Massacre was prompted by the chance to dethrone the then independent Badruddin and simultaneously effect the seizure of the rich island of Banka then belonging to Palembang is difficult to establish for it depends on our reading of the man's character and political philosophy. This, in turn, depends on our interpretation of what was in his mind when he urged Badruddin to "buang habiskan sekali-kali" the Dutch factory in Palembang.

The first commission Raffles sent to Palembang was on November 2, 1811. The letter Raffles sent to the Governor-General in India referring to the Massacre was on March 7, 1812, while the report on the Massacre submitted by Tunku Radin Mohammed and Syed Abu Bakar was on December 13, 1811. In the letter he made no reference to his previous correspondence with Badruddin. He stressed the need to acquire Banka and what he considered to be legitimate British claims by right of conquest. The British, he reasoned, inherited the right to Banka through the Dutch. The Dutch had surrendered its dependency, Palembang. The purpose of the commission was to offer a better deal to the Sultan, according to Raffles. Raffles described the Sultan's reaction in the following manner:

> He not only treated with a kind of ridicule and neglect the claims of the British government to the contracts which subsisted with the former government before the conquest of Java, but rejected with disdain the new terms which were offered to him. The Sultan altogether disregarded the representations on the part of the British government, until he received authentic accounts of the fall of Batavia; and then, instead of listening to the demands of my agents, Toonkoo Radin Mahomet and Syed Abu Bakir, that he should consider the Dutch property and inhabitants as under the protection of the English, who had conquered Java and all its dependencies, he declared in a haughty manner his intention of maintaining his entire independence of any power on earth. Struck, however, by the sudden, and to him cer-

tainly unexpected news, of the complete conquest of Java by the English, the Sultan became anxious for his future fate, and by threats and force compelled my agents to sign and seal false reports, forged by the Sultan and addressed to me, in which it was stated that the Dutch garrison had, agreeably to their request, been sent to Batavia, and the fort razed to the ground, long previous to the attack upon the island of Java by the British troops; and to cover the false-hood of this report (on the faith of which he had laid the foundation of his future independence), he formed the dia-bolical plan of destroying every witness who might here-after appear against him, sending the Dutch inhabitants in small prows down the river, where they were murdered by order of the Sultan, and ordering my agents to appear before him, that they might share the same fate.[19]

The rest of the episode and subsequent happening may be recounted briefly. Badruddin's brother, Ahmad Naja-muddin was installed as Sultan by the British, while Badruddin was dethroned and driven away by force. He was, however, allowed to remain in Palembang. The British-created Sultan, Ahmad Najamuddin signed the treaty and ceded Banka to the British, on May 17, 1812.[20] However, on June 29, 1813 the British Resident Robison, turned his back on Najamuddin and worked for the restoration of Badruddin who was eventually re-installed as Sultan on July 13, 1813.[21] Raffles did not recognize the treaty and the return of Badruddin. Another expedi-tion was sent to re-install Najamuddin. Badruddin was again deposed, one month after his re-installation. After the British left Java, the Dutch in June 1811 re-installed Badruddin. Eventually Badruddin resisted the Dutch encroachment on Palembang, which led to a conflict in which he was defeated.

The affairs around the Palembang Sultanate revealed the entire absence of ethical scruples in the diplomacy of the Dutch or the English. True the Massacre was an inhuman act and those who were responsible among the dignitaries of Palembang evinced no ethical scruples, but the events preceding and following it were generated by a standard of political relation which ignored fundamental ethical scruples. The treaty with Palembang was indirectly and sometimes directly forced upon Palembang both by the Dutch and the British at terms which were not favourable to Palembang. A refusal was usually followed by hostility.

The British views of the Massacre differed somewhat from each other. Gillespie suggested that it was Pangeran Ratu, the Sultan's son, who was responsible for the Massacre.[22] Court could not say for certain whether Badruddin was responsible for the Massacre;[23] while Travers, Raffles' assistant-secretary for military affairs, expressed a genuine sympathy for Badruddin on the occasion of his second dethronement. He was "far from believing all the tales we have heard to his prejudice".[24] Resident Robison believed that Badruddin was not guilty. Having made the investigation on the spot, he concluded that it was very difficult to ascertain the facts. Raffles' responsibility in the

Massacre is just as difficult to prove as Badruddin's guilt. There is gradually a crystallized opinion that Raffles was not entirely free of blame. Robison was perhaps the first to point this out as far as the British side was concerned. On the preceding negotiations with Badruddin, Robison said,

> considering the people with whom [they were] opened, the Agent who had to conduct it on our part, and the whole circumstances of [the] transaction[s], might in some Men's judgment have been considered an extenuation at least of the barbarous offence, if it was even clearly proved that he [Badr'uddin] had committed it.[25]

Bastin believes that Badruddin ordered the Massacre but accommodates Robison's point. He said, "But Robison's point about the extenuation of the guilt must be admitted. For it was Raffles' irresponsibility in making a dubious promise of independence that caused the massacre of the Dutch."[26] The British view of Raffles' responsibility differs from the view current in Dutch circles. The best summary of the Dutch view was given by Levyssohn Norman: "The significance of the words used by Raffles is in its original so broad that every means the Sultan intends to employ to make an end to the Dutch factory, whether it is expulsion, murder or imprisonment, can, in the eyes of the Sultan be given an excuse."[27] His judgement was based on Baud's article. Coolhaas, in his reaction to Wurtzburg's article, stated that he did not believe

Raffles capable of murder, but he thought Raffles "was guilty of using words in such a rash way as to bring the death of innocent people".[28] He further added, "Nevertheless those who consider Raffles guilty of consciously provoking the murder are defending a strong position. For the murder of the Dutch suited Raffles excellently."[29]

Amongst the numerous Dutch scholars who made the attempt to judge Raffles' guilt in the Massacre, Veth is to be mentioned if only because Wurtzburg quoted him as saying that murder was not in keeping with Raffles' character. Owing to Wurtzburg's lack of knowledge of Dutch and his negligence in checking his facts, he did not know that Veth had withdrawn the above statement in 1898, half a century before he was quoted by Wurtzburg.[30] Veth's judgment which Wurtzburg quoted was delivered years before 1898. As the British works on Raffles, with the exception of those of Bastin, cannot be considered as serious scholarship we shall pay more attention to Bastin's view of the Massacre of Palembang. Independent of his conclusions, his article is the most up to date and successful attempt to extend significantly the relevant area of discourse. Some of his arguments are new. The most interesting one is his suggestion that Baud's copy of Raffles' letter containing the sinister passage, "buang habiskan sekali-kali" may not be authentic.[31] This, to my mind, is the only serious argument put forward by Bastin. The remainder of the arguments are weak and, in some instances, uncritical. Before discussing this further I should like to suggest an explanatory framework to pave the way for a theory of Raffles' responsibility regarding the Massacre of Palembang.

In the light of circumstantial and documentary evidence before us Raffles could have been guided by the following motives in his dealings with the Sultanate of Palembang: (1) He consciously and deliberately planned the Massacre with the conscious participation of Badruddin or some influential figures in Palembang. (2) He consciously and deliberately provoked the Massacre without the conscious participation of Badruddin or any of his chiefs, the entire plan being engineered by his men in Palembang. (3) Raffles had no design to massacre the Dutch factory but he was aware that his inflammatory and hateful propaganda against the Dutch might lead to the garrison being massacred. (4) Raffles never for once thought that the garrison would be massacred despite his inflammatory agitation to attack and expel them, and his denouncing the evil of the Dutch.

The attitudes he could have taken towards the Massacre would be (a) approval, (b) indifference, or (c) disapproval. We are not here concerned with the direct overt expression of an attitude both in terms of action or inaction.[32]

Number (4) of the alternatives is excluded by the evidence.

Raffles knew the Dutch garrison was in danger, as early as March 1811 when he asked Captain Macdonald to try

48

and repatriate the Dutch.[33] In March 1811, the Sultan, Badruddin, wrote the following to Raffles:

> We have also been informed with regard to the wishes of our friend respecting your enemies the Hollanders which are in Palembang. Let not our friend have either doubt or fear any longer regarding them, for in truth we will conduct ourselves regarding them with the utmost of our ability, so that everything shall proceed agreeably to the wishes of our friend. Besides with respect to this conduct nothing whether right or wrong shall be concealed, nor shall there be either failure or fault on my part to interfere with our friendship for the future. I have accordingly sent to Batavia that they may take away these Hollanders with all speed who are in Palembang, and if they are not speedy in taking them off, some misfortune will befall them and the blame will not be mine. Such is the state of the matter, but the message has not yet arrived. In this matter however we are not in truth devoid of resources in order to accomplish our purpose with all speed according to the desire of my friend. Let not therefore my friend have any further doubts about these Hollanders, for I have no intercourse nor connection with them.
>
> It is however proper that we should inform our friend concerning the first introduction of the Hollanders into Palembang for in former times they were of great utility to our ancestors, and our ancestors did not wish us to forget their good offices, and thus the Hollanders have continued in Palembang to the present time, but at present we have no connection with them, and no desire to be concerned in the operations of the Hollanders, for they are only aliens in

effect and it is to us that the country belongs. Therefore let not our friend have any doubts regarding them for we will do our best to expel the enemies of our friend.[34]

A few months before that in December 15, 1810, Raffles had incited the Sultan to attack the Dutch and drive them away. He had himself sent Badruddin arms and ammunition for this purpose.

We are thus left with the first three of our alternatives. The first is that Raffles deliberately planned the murder of the garrison. This cannot be established by the evidence at hand. Even Badruddin's guilt is difficult to establish. Bastin's suggestion (based on the explanation of Raffles' agents) that Badruddin's main motive for the Massacre was to claim that Palembang had driven the Dutch out before the surrender of Java, thereby entitling it to an independent status in line with Raffles' reasoning, is certainly difficult to accept. It presumes too much. Why should Badruddin consider it as a threat to his sovereignty if the Dutch moved out and the British came in to replace them? The indications were that Badruddin at that time had sufficient faith in the British. He had signed a treaty with them and would have welcomed the change. To impute such a motive for the Massacre is to reduce the intelligence of Badruddin to that of a simpleton. As he himself stated, if he wanted to massacre them he could have done it earlier.[35]

The second alternative, that Raffles consciously provoked the Massacre without committing himself openly to Badruddin, is equally difficult to establish, though one can marshal more circumstantial allusions to it. This appears to be the view held in certain Dutch circles, although not exactly Baud's view.

The third alternative is that Raffles, aware of the consequences of his campaign against the Dutch, nevertheless proceeded with it, and took no steps to prevent the Massacre of Palembang by way of deed or statement. Badruddin was not told not to kill the Dutch. Raffles did not define the limit of Badruddin's action to drive away the Dutch, knowing full well that a massacre could easily be a consequence of his (Raffles') inflammatory hate campaign against the Dutch. In his letter of February, 1811, from Calcutta, Lord Minto had told Raffles that a sudden transfer of European life and property to the power of Malay chiefs might attract their vengeance.[36] My view is that Raffles, though not guilty of deliberately ordering the Massacre, nevertheless played about with the lives of those in the Dutch garrison. In many respects this view supports Baud's.[37] Raffles' activity preceding and following the Massacre expressed an amoral political philosophy but as he was a member of an amoral generation of empire-builders, big and small, he was not alone in holding to this philosophy.

To establish the above view it is necessary to demolish Bastin's presentation of Raffles' case. Bastin accepted Raffles' partial responsibility for the Massacre, but on totally different grounds. It was the promise of independence for Badruddin if he succeeded in expelling the Dutch, and not the rifles supplied, and the agitations of hatred against the Dutch which are the correct grounds. I have earlier noted that this explanation seems to be rather far-fetched. Leaving this aside, Bastin seems to be partial in his selection of reliable sources: his entire explanation is dominated by the statement made by Tunku Radin Mohammed and Syed Abu Bakar, Raffles' two agents. He ignores Robison's warning that these two gentlemen were untrustworthy characters. I am inclined to give more weight to Robison's judgement for there are some enigmatic circumstances surrounding the two agents. Bastin does not raise the issue. It seems rather odd that the two gentlemen reported the Massacre in Malacca three months after the alleged date of the Massacre, September 14, 1811. (The report was made on December 12, 1811). The two agents left Palembang about twelve or fourteen days after September 14, 1811. It did not take six weeks to reach Malacca. A week was more than sufficient. What did the two gentlemen do? Their own report was that they were then running for their lives.

Their report was signed in Malacca on December 13, 1812, before the Commissioned Members of the Court of Justice. Raffles received this report on December 18, while he received the report from the Commission he sent to Palembang on December 13.[38] There appears to have been some haste in obtaining the report of his two agents after they had taken their time in returning to Malacca. Could it be that the report of December 13, 1812, was prepared to conform with Raffles' official line of explanation? In other words is it that it was not a true account of the happening? We have reason to be critical about this document because the entire British case to justify the dethronement of Badruddin and the enthronement of Najamuddin was based on it.[39] As van der Kemp said, Raffles was a man who would twist and turn at all corners. The two agents accused Badruddin's son, Pangeran Ratu, of forcing them to send a letter to Raffles.[40] Robison doubted the honesty of the agent Tunku Radin Mohammed who, he claimed, had fabricated many lies. Furthermore Pangeran Ratu was never employed in public business by the Sultan.[41]

The Malacca Report of December 13, 1812, contains some questionable elements, reinforcing the suspicion that the report was a frame-up against the Sultan of Palembang. Only two dates were given, that of the agents' arrival at Minto (Muntok) on July 22, 1811, and the date of the Massacre (September 14, 1811). Other significant dates were sequentially described. The following phrases were used: "after having been some time in Palembang", "eight days more", "three days after this", "six days after", "having been three days at Soensang". The reconstructed chronology of events based on the report would then be the following, taking September 14 and July 22 as the reference points:

July 22, 1811, arrival of the two agents at Minto. Some days later, they were invited to proceed to Palembang. By September 3, 1811, a vessel arrived at Palembang with news of the Dutch surrender, but the news was discredited by the Sultan. By September 11, 1811, Syed Zain Balfagih arrived from Semarang with news of the Dutch surrender and the news was accepted by the Sultan. The Massacre of the Dutch garrison was on September 14, 1811. The two agents saw the Dutch garrison demolished on September 17, 1811, and on September 23, the two agents were summoned by the Sultan but instead were received by Pangeran Ratu, Badruddin's son, who forced them to sign the letter which they disowned in the Malacca Report. From September 26 to 30, 1811, they were permitted to stay in Sunsang and thereafter fled for their lives to Malacca.

From the Malacca Report some serious questions arise. It is strange that Bastin (and other defenders of Raffles) had not found it necessary to apply the canons of historical criticism to this report. If the report were true, and not an official fabrication to cover up Raffles' intrigues against the Dutch and to put the blame on Badruddin, why did the two agents linger for more than three months before submitting it?

It was on November 2, 1811, that Raffles sent his first mission to Palembang after the Dutch surrender. This mission consisted of Wardenaar, Hare, and Captain Phillips. The Malacca Report would like us to believe that

Raffles knew nothing of the Massacre yet. It would like us to believe that the two agents of Raffles were lingering somewhere for one month, the whole of October, without reporting to Raffles until finally on December 12, Farquhar ordered them to submit their report and to declare the facts therein as real and true. According to this "ordered declaration" they arrived from Palembang on December 7, 1811. According to the same report, after translating the sequential reference "having been 3 days at Soensang" they left Palembang somewhere between September 26 and 30, 1811. Where were they between September 30 and December 7, 1811? They were supposed to be running for their lives. They claimed that they had safely obtained a boat to escape from Palembang and carried valuable information on the events at Palembang. They were Raffles' responsible agents. They claimed a letter had been forged with their seals on it, but if this were the case would they have kept silent for three months as though nothing had happened? Or did they perhaps report the matter and then remain quiet until Farquhar ordered them to submit an officially written report so that Raffles could make use of it as a justification for his action against Palembang and his official explanation of his involvement in the Palembang affair?

The most interesting part of the Malacca Report is the claim that the letter noted was a forgery. The letter, in English, reads:

Warkat al-ikhlas, from Tunku Sharif Mohammed to our
friend Mr Raffles. We arrived at Muntok on the 18th day
of Rajab. We received news from our friend that the Dutch
had been driven out by Tuan Seri Paduka Sultan. We
ordered people to go to Palembang and check this news and
it was really so. Nothing was left, cleanly finished. In all
respects, it was in accordance with the desire of our friend.
Concerning the envoy of Tuan Seri Paduka Sultan Ratu we
are told that he is in Java. What if we receive no more news?
We request our friend's assistance to see that he returns
immediately to Palembang. Such is the situation. On our
arrival at Muntok we sent an earlier letter by a small boat
informing you of the same news as contained in this one.
Written on 28 Sha'aban, 1226.

The original letter in Romanized Malay is as follows:

Warkat al-akhlas daripada Tunku Sharif Mohammed sampai kapada sahabat kita Master Raffles. Maka adalah kita
sampai ke Muntok kapada delapan belas hari bulan Rejab.
Dapat khabar dari [?] sahabat kita Hollanders sudah dikelu-
arkan Tuan Seri Paduka Sultan. Maka kita suroh orang
pergi periksa melihat khabar itu kedalam Palembang. Maka
sunggohlah saperti itu. Sudah tiada apa lagi yang tinggal,
habis bersih. Pada sekalian keadaannya itu, telah saperti
maksud sahabat kita adanya. Maka akan utusan Tuan Seri
Paduka Sultan Ratu kita dapat khabar, lagi ada tinggal di
Tanah Djawa. Apa halnya tiada boleh lagi khabar
melainkan kita pinta dengan penolong sahabat kita supaya
segera pulang ke Palembang. Demikianlah adanya. Sha-
hadan waktu sampai kita ke Muntok sudah ada satu surat
kita kirimkan dahulu daripada surat ini dengan sabuah per-

ahu kechil, mengkhabarkan saperti mana perkhabaran ini
jua adanya. Tersurat pada dua lapan likur bulan Sha'aban,
1226.

This letter to Raffles is claimed by the two agents to be
a forgery. In the report they submitted by order of Farquhar, the letter was rendered thus:

> This letter comes from Toenko Sereef, Mahomet to my
> friend Mr T. S. Raffles. I have to communicate to my friend
> my arrival at Minto on the 18th of the month of Redjab, or
> the 5th of August last, and that I have received tidings that
> the enemies of my friend (the Dutch) have been sent away
> by the Sultan – I have sent people thither, and they have
> confirmed it, and that no signs of them are left. I also have
> learned, that there are ambassadors from Palembang at Java.
> I request you to assist these people, that they may be enabled
> speedily to return. My letter, the original of this, sent to you
> from Minto, I hope you received in due time.[42]

As certain parts from the original Malay letter were
deleted the above translation is not accurate. In the version of the Malacca Report the following words were·
deleted: "Nothing was left, cleanly finished. In all respects,
it was in accordance with the desire of our friend."
("Sudah tiada apa lagi yang tinggal, habis bersih. Pada
sekalian keadaannya itu, telah seperti maksud sahabat kita
adanya".) The exclusion of the above sentences from the
official Malacca Report lends further plausibility to our
suspicion that the report was unreliable. Why was that

part of the letter omitted which revealed the degree and
nature of Raffles' intrigue further? The omission pointed
to the fact that Raffles desired more than merely sending
the Dutch away. The party that stands to benefit in the
deletion of this part of the letter was definitely that of Raffles and his British colleagues.

The claim that this letter was a forgery signed by
Tunku Sharif Mohammed under compulsion by the Sultan's son, Pangeran Ratu becomes even more dubious if
one bears in mind the reference to an original copy sent
from Minto (Muntok). If the letter was drafted by the
Sultan's party where was the need for them to point to
an original copy sent earlier elsewhere? This would only
increase the possibility of exposure? It implied that there
were two forged letters instead of one. It could easily
be discovered that the Minto letter was not sent by Raffles' agents. How did the Sultan obtain the seal of Tunku
Sharif Mohammed on the letter from Minto? There was
no suggestion whatsoever that the two agents were likewise seized in Minto and compelled to write a letter to
Raffles. If that was the case why did they not escape
immediately thereafter? Instead they willingly went to
seek an audience with the Sultan and allowed themselves
to be forced for the second time, negating the Dutch saying "Een ezel stapt niet tweemal op de zelfde steen" or
"A donkey does not step twice on the same stone." The
agent Tunku Sharif Mohammed was thus even more stu-

pid than a donkey. It implied that Raffles was equally stupid for employing such a stupid agent.

Considering all the points above it becomes more plausible to consider that Raffles with the assistance of Farquhar engaged himself in preparing his own version of the record of the relations with the Sultan of Palembang. They prepared the official British record to cover up the past intrigues and to be used as a basis in the dispute with the Dutch should the occasion arise. The occasion did arise after the British withdrawal from Java. Baud's article of 1852 was not the first intimation of the Dutch view on Raffles' intrigues. In December 1814 the news had leaked out in Batavia. In 1817, for instance, Goldberg warned the Dutch king that it was dangerous to let the British have Benkulen with Raffles there. He noted Raffles' behaviour with reference to the Massacre of Palembang in 1811.[43] Raffles had strong reasons to prepare an official defence of his conduct with reference to Palembang as he was aware that Badruddin was using his letters to defend his position. Since the Massacre had already taken place there was nothing left to do but to put the defence in such a framework of explanation that would eliminate the personal elements of Raffles' diplomacy and shift the emphasis entirely on Badruddin's desire for independence together with the appropriate chronology of events. It must be remembered that the date of the Massacre, September 14, 1811, is entirely based on the Malacca Report. Other earlier sources did not mention the date. The letter repudiated by the Malacca Report was dated 28 Sha'aban 1226 A.H. or September 20, 1811.[44] The Malay text given above noted that an earlier letter informing of the same news was sent from Minto (Muntok). This meant that the news of the Massacre could have been sent long before September 14, 1811.

In April 1821, at Tjianjur, West Java, Najamuddin offered his account of the Massacre to Baud and van der Capellen. No date or month was mentioned.[45] An eye-witness, Willem van de Weteringe Buis, mentioned December 29, 1811 as the date but another, a widow, mentioned no date. As the Massacre was not fully explained and details were hidden, nobody ever suggested a definite and reliable date. The date later writers used was the one suggested in the Malacca Report, and this was the only official report available. Fixing the date as September 14, 1811, after the capitulation of Batavia on August 26, 1811, would fit in with the official British explanation and justification for the subsequent deposition of Badruddin. No one of Badruddin's group would be in the position to deny the date since a denial meant knowledge of the Massacre and an eventual accusation of complicity. Hence it would be quite safe to fix the date but for the contradictions and inconsistencies in the narration of the two agents. They claimed the Massacre to have taken place on 27 Sha'aban 1226 A.H., and on the next day they claimed to have been compelled to write the repudiated letter. If this was the case why should the Sultan's son, Pangeran

Ratu, as noted earlier, make them send a letter, more than a week before the date of the Massacre, informing Raffles of the Massacre? Assuming that the Sultan's party managed to steal the seal of Tunku Sharif Mohammed, then returning it to him without his knowledge (after using it to send a forged letter), why should they go to this trouble?

Circumstantial evidence points to the fact that the letter in Raffles' collection, repudiated in the Malacca Report is not a false communication by the Sultan's son as alleged by the two agents. It was Raffles' two agents who concealed the truth and made a false and convenient allegation against the Sultan of Palembang.[46] The letter they repudiated was the only available evidence that the Massacre took place before September 14, 1811, presumably even before August 26, 1811. It had to be repudiated because Badruddin was likely to have a copy of it. By the time the Malacca Report was drawn up, it was known in Batavia that Badruddin had shown Raffles' letters to the mission sent by Raffles. Phillips, Hare, and Wardenaar, the three members of the mission were shown the letters on November 25, 1811. They arrived in Batavia in early December. Their report to Raffles was dated December 6, 1811. They must have reached Batavia earlier as they left Palembang immediately after November 25. There was thus time to summon the two agents to submit the Malacca Report which would eventually be used as the document to justify the dethronement of Badruddin.

There is further another unexplained problem. What was the Sultan's motive in fabricating a letter informing Raffles that the Dutch had been forced to disappear without indicating any date? Badruddin told the commission that he did not inform Raffles of the elimination of the Dutch fort because Raffles had not asked him to do so. The date was a significant factor in the British interpretation of Badruddin's motive. He could have easily inserted a date, say one before the Dutch surrender at Batavia (August 26, 1811). In appraising the issue we should make a distinction between Badruddin's responsibility regarding the Massacre and his fabrication of the letter repudiated by the Malacca Report. As I suggested earlier it is more plausible to consider the report that lied rather than the letter. To my mind the letter was authentic, sent by Raffles' agent. It was Raffles and the British authority who had a perfect motive for disowning the letter. That letter showed clearly that Raffles was desirous of eliminating the Dutch garrison. It was written with allusive sentences which could be construed as a confirmation of Raffles' involvement in the Massacre. If this letter could be disowned, others, too, could be similarly treated.

Bastin attempted to deny the reliability of Raffles' letter to Badruddin used by Baud where the words "buang, habiskan sekali-kali" occurred.[47] Instead he prefers to rely on Raffles' Malay version of the letter, found in his collection. The letter in Raffles' possession carried the words "pukul buang sekali-kali". The version used by Baud had a sinister meaning. Bastin also noted the original English copy of the letter. To interpret Raffles' motives Bastin suggests that we use the English draft of the letter, not the Malay draft. He said, "For the moment it is important to point out that Raffles did not actually pen any of the Malay letters to Palembang himself. He gave English drafts to his scribe who put them into Malay. It is therefore necessary, if we are to examine Raffles' motives in his negotiations, to consider these English drafts rather than their Malay translations. Fortunately most of these drafts have been preserved in the India Office Library, London. With these and other English translations of Malay letters sent by Badruddin to Raffles in reply, we can now build up a satisfactory account of Raffles' negotiations with Palembang prior to the Java invasion."[48]

The following implications arise from Bastin's remarks: (a) The version used by Baud was not reliable. (b) The English original was the reliable and reasonable one to use as the basis on which to judge Raffles. (c) Badruddin, the Sultan of Palembang, used an unreliable version of Raffles' letter to defend his conduct and press his claim on the throne of Palembang. (d) The Dutch used the same materials to put the blame on the British. (e) There could not be more than one version of the letter which Raffles actually sent.

If these implications are acceptable then only can we consider Bastin's attempt to disprove Baud's explanation as successfully accomplished. As they stand now, it seems to me that Bastin's suggestion and its implications will not survive the logic of historical interpretation. To begin with, why should we rely on the British original? Surely Raffles would not include such phrases in the English original, assuming the fact that he was a cautious intriguer. As to Badruddin we would have to consider him a simpleton for using an unauthentic document to press his claim for the throne of Palembang! As to the different styles and versions of the letter, why should it not be probable that Raffles employed more than one scribe who might have provided two translations of the same letter or content?

The above considerations compel us to view Raffles' conduct against the Sultanate of Palembang as one of expansionistic intrigues without regard to their consequence to others. Though we have no available and convincing proofs as to his instigation of the Massacre, he was responsible nevertheless for writing inflammatory letters, the consequences of which could easily have been anticipated by him. Responsibility for the Massacre cannot be put upon the shoulders of Badruddin alone. In the matter of proofs, it is equally difficult to obtain convincing proofs as to the guilt of Badruddin in ordering the Massacre. One thing is certain, the Massacre had taken place, and some people were responsible, and to some extent Raffles was. British writers on Raffles had painted a progressive if not saintly portrait of him. They have entirely ignored his ideas on certain subjects and his general philosophy. To understand Raffles and to evaluate the significance of the changes he introduced it is essential that we relate them to his general outlook. His general chauvinistic British philosophy explains why he was enthusiastic in agitating in his letters to the Sultan of Palembang for the liquidation of the Dutch garrison without concern as to the likely consequence of his correspondence.

Raffles' Views on the Different Communities in this Area

Raffles' opinion on the different communities in this area reveals what is now called in the social sciences "ethnic prejudice" or "communal prejudice". It is perhaps fortunate that in Singapore Raffles is known by the general public only as the administrative and commercial founder of the island. He is also known as a person who loved scholarship and was fond of the Malay language. His writings on the different communities are not widely known. On the Malays he had the following to say:

> The Malay, living in a country where nature grants (almost without labour) all his wants, is so indolent, that when he has rice, nothing will induce him to work. Accustomed to

wear arms from his infancy, to rely on his own prowess for safety, and to dread that of his associates, he is the most correctly polite of all savages, and not subject to those starts of passion so common to more civilized nations. But with all his forbearance, he is feelingly alive to insult; submits with a bad grace to the forms to which, in a civilized life, he finds himself obliged to conform; and when these are either numerous or enforced with supercilious contumely, or the delays of office, he flies to the woods, where, with a little rice boiled in a bamboo, eaten with sprouts of the surrounding trees as a leaf, he feels he is free.[1]

Raffles considered the Malays degraded owing to the exploitation of the Dutch and the Asiatics such as the Chinese and the Arabs, as well as their own rulers. The British were, in his opinion, best suited to reform the Malays and bring justice and prosperity. Some of his opinions and discussions on the Malays are quite interesting and on the whole he was sympathetic to the Malays as long as they did not cause him trouble. The same could be said of his attitude to the Chinese. As long as they worked under British administration serving the interest of the status quo Raffles was content with them. But when the Chinese acted against his interests he wrote: "The Chinese, in all ages equally supple, venal, and crafty, failed not at a very early period to recommend themselves to the equally crafty, venal, and speculating Hollanders. They have, almost from the first, been the agents of the Dutch, and in the island of Java, in particular, they have almost acquired the entire monopoly of revenue farms and government contracts."[2] The British government was warned against the Chinese. "Although the Chinese, as being the most diligent and industrious settlers, should be the most useful, they are, on the contrary, become a very dangerous people, and are to be remarked as a pest to the country; and that there appears to be no radical cure for this evil but their extermination from the interior, a measure which cannot now be effected."[3]

Raffles' policy towards the Chinese is revealing in its tone and motivation. He reacted to them rather strongly and it is best to quote him at length to illustrate his bias:

Wherever they have formed extensive settlements in Java, accordingly, the native Javanese have no alternative but that of abandoning the district, or becoming slaves of the soil; besides the monopolizing spirit of the Chinese frequently exercises a very pernicious control over the necessaries of life, and the produce of the soil, even in the vicinity of Batavia. If we consider the suppleness and insinuating address of the Chinese, how apt they are on all occasions to curry favour, how ready they are to proffer assistance when there is no danger, and when they perceive that it falls in with their own interest, we may depend upon their utmost efforts being used to ingratiate themselves with the English. It is, therefore, of the greatest importance to be early on our guard against this pernicious and increasing influence, which preys on the very vitals of the country, draining and exhausting it for the benefit of China. In all the Malay states, the Chinese have made every effort to get into their hands the farming of the port duties, and this has generally proved the ruin of the trade. In addition to these circumstances, it should be recollected that the Chinese, from their peculiar language and manners, form a kind of separate society in every place where they settle, which gives them great advantage over every competitor in arranging monopolies of trade. It also gives them an opportunity of aspiring after political ascendancy, which they have often acquired in the inferior Malay states. This ascendancy of the Chinese, whether of a commercial or political nature, should be cautiously guarded against and restrained; and this perhaps cannot be better done than by bringing forward the native population of Malays and Javanese, and encouraging them in useful and industrious habits.[4]

The Arabs were likewise severely condemned by Raffles of whom he said:

The Chinese must, at all events, be admitted to be industrious; but the Arabs are mere drones, useless and idle consumers of the produce of the ground, affecting to be descendants of the Prophet, and the most eminent of his followers, when in reality they are commonly nothing more than manumitted slaves: they worm themselves into the favour of the Malay chiefs, and often procure the highest offices in the Malay states. They hold like robbers the offices they obtain as sycophants, and cover all with the sanctimonious veil of religious hypocrisy. Under the pretext of instructing the Malays in the principles of the Mahomedan religion, they inculcate the most intolerant bigotry, and render them incapable of receiving any species of useful knowledge.[5]

Raffles' intense dislike for the Arabs extended to the Islamic religion which he called the "robber-religion".[6] To diminish the influence of Islam Raffles suggested the propagation of Christianity. He was perturbed by the tenacious hold of Islam on the Muslims and he saw a political danger to British power in the defiant attitude of Islam. The following is an instance he furnished:

> In our present settlement of Malacca, the impossibility of procuring servants for wages compels almost every person to have recourse to slaves, and a considerable proportion of these are Pagans, being chiefly Battas from the centre of Sumatra, Balis from Bali, Dayaks from Borneo, besides natives of Timor and the more easterly islands. Of all these slaves that fall into the hands, of the English, there is perhaps not a single one that becomes a Christian, but the whole of them become Moslems, and despise and hate their masters as infidels. Such is the woeful effect of our supineness and indifference, which, if they should extend to the East, would certainly not tend to the progress of general improvement among the Malays.[7]

In addition to the Dutch, the Chinese and the Arabs, Raffles also disliked the Americans whom he described as "another class of commercial interlopers who will require our vigilant attention."[8] The Americans could become a serious competitor of the English. Already they had frequented several islands of the East Indies, and they also had hired their vessels to the Dutch. "The Americans," he said, "wherever they go, as they have no object but commercial adventure, and as firearms are in the highest request, especially among the more Eastern isles, these would be considered as the most profitable articles. They have already filled the different clusters of islands in the South Seas with firearms, and they would not fail to do the same in the different Eastern islands."[9] In Raffles' view, the Americans together with the Chinese and the Arabs should not be allowed to trade on equal terms with the English. Having discussed the nature of each group and their relation to English interest, Raffles suggested to Lord Minto the significance of conquering the area for the English. He said, "It may, however, be stated generally, that the acquisition of the Dutch possessions in the East places the command of the spice trade, together with that of pepper and coffee, besides a variety of other eastern produce, entirely in our hands, and that the Continent must either do without these articles, or submit to purchase them from the English."[10]

As apparent from the above, Raffles' likes and dislikes towards the different groups were motivated by the degree and nature each of them affected English interests. His sympathies, his prejudices, and his actions were all based on English imperial interests more than anything else. Neither the philosophy of the Enlightenment nor Christian values played a dominant role in his thinking.

His was the typical philosophy of the empire builder, the 19th-century chauvinist, the Machiavellian imperialist. His counterpart was to be found among the Dutch, the French, the Spaniards, and the Portuguese. They differ in methods and attitudes towards the conquered peoples but they share a common basic philosophy characterized by the following traits: (1) the world had progressed and developed putting the European nations at the top, (2) the European nations had the right to inherit the earth, to conquer and subjugate other parts of the world in the interest of imperialistic capitalism, (3) the other parts of the world had to be civilized according to European standards, (4) ethical scruples could be overruled by the interest of one's own nation. Raffles was one of the many imperialist personalities of 19th-century Europe. A characteristic feature of Raffles, his ambivalence towards certain issues, is best explained by illustration.

Those people whom he found defiant, dangerous, or competitive to the English he disliked and this dislike expanded to their religion, culture, and daily practices. On the other hand to those who were weak, fruitful, or friendly to the English, he would express his sympathy and tolerance to a remarkable degree. His bigoted attitude towards the Chinese, the Arabs, and the Dutch stands in sharp contrast with his remarkable tolerance towards the Bugis, the people of Nias, and the Bataks. In his letter to William Marsden, February 27, 1820, he described how he assembled some Batak chiefs and inquired the state of cannibalism in their society. Cannibalism was a form of punishment for adultery, midnight robbery, intermarriage in the same tribe, and treacherous attack. In addition to these it was practised against prisoners in important wars, the wars of one district against another. The victim was tied to a stake with extended arms encircled by a group. If it was for a crime the chief enemy or the aggrieved party would be the first to cut off a slice from the victim's body the moment the chief gave the order to commence.

The others cut off their pieces and ate these pieces either raw or roasted. The victim was not killed until the whole of the flesh was eaten. Thereafter the head was cut off and taken home by the chief or the injured party. Having given a detailed and glowing description of cannibalism and its function in Batak society, Raffles said,

> I have also a great deal to say on the other side of the character, for the Battas have many virtues. I prize them highly. However horrible eating a man may sound in European ears, I question whether the party suffers so much, or the punishment itself is worse than the European tortures of two centuries ago. I have always doubted the policy, and even the right of capital punishment among civilized nations; but this once admitted, and torture allowed, I see nothing more cruel in eating a man alive than in torturing him for days with mangled limbs and the like. Here they certainly eat him up at once, and the party seldom suffers

73

more than a few minutes. It is probable that he suffers more pain from the loss of his ear than from what follows: indeed he is said to give one shriek when that is taken off, and then to continue silent till death.[11]

He recognized the effectiveness of the punishment. In the area around Tapanuli two people had been eaten within the last three years when Raffles was there. On the effect of this punishment Raffles said, "These severe punishments certainly tend to prevent crimes. The Battas are honest and honourable, and possess many more virtues that I have time to put down".[12] He praised the Bataks' devotion to the law more than the Muslims' to the Quran. Bearing in mind how calmly and dispassionately he treated the subject of Batak cannibalism as an effective deterrent against crime, and the almost apologetic tone with which he compared the practice with certain European forms of punishment, we need not wonder the ease with which Raffles hung the mutilated body of Syed Yasin for display in Singapore in an iron cage specially and hurriedly built by him for that occasion.

Syed Yasin was imprisoned by Farquhar for not paying a debt he owed to another trader. One evening, on the pretext of looking for his creditor to settle the matter, he was taken out. On reaching the creditor's house he broke loose and killed the police guard. The creditor escaped to Farquhar's house. Farquhar and a party of men searched the creditor's house. Syed Yasin sprang upon

Farquhar, stabbing at the breast. Syed Yasin was struck by Farquhar's son with a sword, and his jaw was split from mouth to ear, causing immediate death. This retribution was not enough for Raffles. He had the mutilated corpse strung up in an iron cage, carried in a bullock cart around the town and then hung up on a pole at Telok Ayer. The deteriorated, dehydrated and mutilated corpse was displayed for 15 days, according to Abdullah.[13] After this, on the Sultan's request, Raffles ceded the body. The funeral prayer and ceremony were then performed. Raffles' action was offensive to the Muslims' conscience. According to Islam the dead must be buried respectfully and religiously as soon as possible no matter what the previous crime was. According to Nahuijs this action of Raffles created tension among the Malays. During the days of display the population lived in a tense atmosphere with their weapons ready.[13] As the killer was already killed in return there was no need to hang his body for display.

4

The Banjarmasin Affair

The British biographers of Raffles, in their eagerness to portray him as a hero, omitted from their works those aspects of Raffles' life which were not in harmony with their design. They refrained from mentioning, or explained away in only a few sentences such instances as the Banjarmasin Affair and the Sukabumi land deal in which Raffles was involved. The Banjarmasin Affair, or as it was called by some British officials in Java, the Banjarmasin Enormity, reveals the despotic aspect of Raffles' character which cannot be qualified as enlightened or humane either by our present moral standard or that of his time. The affair centred around the establishment of a peculiar English settlement by Raffles' friend, Alexander Hare, with Raffles' support, at Banjarmasin. Between

1809 and 1811 the coastal areas of Borneo were abandoned by all European powers. After the British occupation of Java Raffles appointed Alexander Hare Commissioner and Resident of Banjarmasin allegedly at the invitation of the Sultan.

In 1811 Hare brought about a contract with the Sultan of Banjarmasin for the British acquisition of a territory along south, southeast, east and northeast of the Borneo coast.[1] In addition to this he acquired personally from the Sultan a grant of 1,400 square miles of land. As noted by William Boggie, a former British Resident of Semarang, who was sent to investigate this affair by Raffles' successor, Fendall, after Raffles was transferred from Java, this unprecedented and indecent transaction was sanctioned and approved by Raffles.[2] It was generally known that all British officials were not allowed to receive personal gifts from the princes with whom they were in official relationship.

Baud cited the case of James Brooke, when he was the British Consul to a sultanate in Borneo. He had to transfer the gift of a coal mine to the Borneo Company.[3] Hare was allowed to retain this gift for grant of 1,400 acres. Subsequently, after the Dutch return to Java, Raffles wrote to the Dutch Governor Baron van der Capellen from Benkulen in June 1818, informing him that Alexander Hare was trying to tender to the British Government a "tract of land and territorial rights" alienated to him by the Sultan of Banjarmasin. By Raffles' own admission the

1,400 sq. miles, an area 6½ times Singapore, was the private possession of his friend Alexander Hare.

In his address to the Batavian Society of Arts and Sciences, April 23, 1813, he had the following to say of his friend Alexander Hare:

> Much valuable and interesting information has already been collected by Mr Alexander Hare, the present Resident, a gentleman whose desire after useful knowledge and whose zealous exertions in the cause he has undertaken, are perhaps unrivalled, and from the progress which he has already made in developing the general nature of the country and character of its inhabitants, the happiest results may be contemplated. He has already made several incursions, and projects at an early period penetrating far into the interior of the country. Under his enlightened administration the country subjected to Banjer Masin has been already reduced to order and regulation, and it is reasonable to expect that the shores of all Borneo may in time be approached without danger, and the population of the interior open to safe and general communication.[4]

What had Alexander Hare done to accomplish his "enlightened administration" of the area?

Hare controlled the area in the manner of a petty despot with the help of his friend Raffles. The establishment was a flop. The British themselves eventually became alarmed. No sooner was Raffles removed from Java in the beginning of 1816, when his successor, Fendall, sent William Boggie to investigate the affair.

What alarmed the authority was not merely the inefficiency of Hare's private colony, but the fact that it was an unprofitable venture.[5] What was most disturbing was the manner in which Hare obtained his labour supply. With Raffles' assistance Hare obtained forced labour from Java and requested that Raffles provide him with a population. Accordingly Raffles sent Hare the population required: first he sent convicts and Hare was given 25 rupiahs for the monthly subsistence of each convict; later this allowance was reduced and eventually stopped.[6] The transport was effected mostly by ships owned by Hare. Van Boeckholtz, who was there in 1816, noted that Hare attempted to create a village organization. According to him the settlement failed despite Raffles' great assistance because of Hare's frequent absences, when he went to Batavia, and because of the waste of labour employed in non-essential undertakings. An example cited was the construction of Hare's residence which was designed to be higher than the tallest tree and had 1,650 poles. More than 100 men worked for 20 months to build this house. Around this were the houses of the women members of the colony.

Raffles first issued the official instruction on May 31, 1813 but apparently on April 25, 18 15, there was a need to clarify the instructions further. In this instruction, three classes of people were mentioned: (1) convicts sentenced by courts whose punishment included transportation; (2) those who were sentenced for lesser offences not involving transportation to other areas; and (3) those who could be induced to go as colonists. However, force was also applied to the third group. Referring to the second and third groups, Assey's instruction contains the following: "The two latter classes forfeit no right of which they ever possessed. They proceed either voluntarily, or are removed from temptation to crime and placed in a situation where they may be induced to earn an honest livelihood, and it is not considered proper that in embarking for Banjarmasin they should be subjected to the penalties and privations which the Law directs for convicts."[7] The use of force was justified with the excuse of removing from temptation to crime those considered as vagrants. Hare, in a memorandum to the government urged, through the village chiefs to persuade ladies to emigrate to his establishment by means of financial reward. However, those women of loose morals should be transported against their will. Hare suggested that this group were easy to identify and reward money need not be spent on them.[8]

In a report of July 31, 1816, Hare informed the authorities at Batavia of the number of people in his settlement. There were 907 men of whom 809 were under life sentence and the rest under sentence ranging from 1 to 25 years. There were 462 women and 123 children. His remark on the women is worth noting:

Of the women 80 are from sentences, 137 who have

accompanied their husbands and the remainder have not
brought lists of sentence, but have been sent for bad conduct and are included here as connected now by marriage;
some of them also having come voluntarily and none being
registered. The names of both sexes have been so frequently
changed and the list so deficient and irregular, that the
above list is more formed by inquiry, than from documents,
though all of which have come to hand are preserved.[3]

As is apparent from the above the forceful deportation of
innocent people was clearly admitted. There was never
any dispute about the fact. Raffles' edict made it clear
that he was assisting Hare in procuring people particularly women, who were not under sentence. He did this
not only because of his personal friendship with Hare but
also because he thought it important to have a British settlement in Banjarmasin which could be retained without
reference to the war in Europe. Should the Dutch regain
Java, Banjarmasin could be kept by the British.

That the settlement was running at a loss and ineffi-
ciently maintained was clear at the time. The accountant, J. G. Bauer, had indicated this.[10] After the transfer
(or removal) of Raffles from Java the Banjarmasin Affair
could no longer be concealed. Java was effectively
restored to the Dutch by August 1816. Fendall, Raffles'
successor, took up his post in March 1816 and it was he
who initiated the investigation of the Banjarmasin settlement though the main object was not an investigation
of Hare's conduct initially; it was carried out with refer-

ence to the problems emerging from the Dutch restoration in Java. The Banjarmasin Affair disclosed one aspect of Raffles' philosophy which has hitherto been deliberately ignored by his admirers. He was capable of violating his own principles by ordering the seizure of innocent persons suspected of eventual criminality. Raffles' edict provided an outlet for kidnapping under the camouflage of the law. Its effect can be imagined. Of the 462 women mentioned by Hare, 245 had been kidnapped, or to put in a mild form, "have been sent for bad conduct". It is beyond doubt that Raffles consciously had deliberately issued the order that enabled those women to be seized and for them to be brought to Banjarmasin. Hare later established himself as the despot of Cocos Island. His interest in women and his unconventional life had provoked some of his British contemporaries. If the term "adventurer" in the derogatory sense requires a fitting embodiment, it is Alexander Hare. Without the assistance of Raffles, Hare would probably not have succeeded in establishing an ill-fated settlement populated by convicts and kidnapped people, ruled by him in the style of a despot with an unbridled passion for women.[11]

5

Raffles and the Ideology of
Imperialism

The Massacre at Palembang and Banjarmasin Affair show that
Raffles was neither the humanitarian he was as presented by
his British admirers, nor was he the scoundrel some Dutch
writers thought he was. As far as Singapore is concerned the
problem is the exaggeration of his so-called good qualities
rather than their opposites. This exaggeration reveals the
naive and docile attitude which exists towards colonial his-
toriography. The British on the whole wrote a propaganda
history of Singapore and Raffles. The exaggeration of Raffles
serves the need for colonial myth making. As long as Raffles is
considered as a historical figure of the colonial past, an administrator of an expansionist government, a person interested in

furthering his career, a man with both insights and prejudices, one who had introduced some changes primarily to benefit his own government, there is no danger in creating a false image of the man and his role in this part of the world. The danger is to consider Raffles as the great humanitarian reformer worthy of respect and adulation, as his widow wanted us to believe. British writers on Raffles have never entirely escaped the influence of his widow's portrayal of her husband.

His role in the history of Singapore has also been exaggerated. Singapore was his last and most insignificant post. From Lieutenant-Governor of Java, he became Lieutenant-Governor of Benkulu, and then of Singapore. Raffles' interests lay more with Sumatra than with Singapore. As far as Singapore was concerned, had Raffles not been around another man would have done the job. If we were to look for the major forces in the development of Singapore they were the following: (1) the consent of the Sultan of Johore to establish Singapore as a port under the British and his refusal to side with the Dutch against the British; (2) Raffles' initial preparation and the even more important subsequent administration of the British; (3) the Asian trade; (4) the immigrant and native population of Singapore; and (5) the Dutch role in Indonesia with its economic exploitation of the country greatly contributing to the entrepot trade of Singapore. Without the Dutch East Indies and the Asian trade Singapore would not have developed as it had. In this particular historical configuration, the person of Raffles was not a very significant element, but in Java and Sumatra he wielded more significant power and was left practically on his own taking many important decisions in advance of his superior's approval. The establishment of Singapore was closely followed by his superiors, but nevertheless Raffles had personally urged the establishment of Singapore.

Raffles' motive for establishing Singapore was to check Dutch supremacy in the area. But for his Malay studies he would not have discovered Singapura, a child of his own. In his letter to Colonel Aldenbrooke, June 10, 1819, Raffles expressed his entire view on Singapore:

> I am sure you will wish me success; and I will therefore only add, that if my plans are confirmed at home, it is my intention to make this my principal residence, and to devote the remaining years of my stay in the East to the advancement of a colony which, in every way in which it can be viewed, bids fair to be one of the most important, and at the same time, one of the least expensive and troublesome, which we possess. Our object is not territory, but trade; a great commercial emporium, and a fulcrum, whence we may extend our influence politically as circumstances may hereafter require. By taking immediate possession, we put a negative to the Dutch claim of exclusion, and at the same time revive the drooping confidence of our allies and friends. One free port in these seas must eventually destroy the spell of Dutch monopoly; and what Malta is in the West, that may Singapore become in the East.[1]

To destroy the Dutch monopoly, to have a base for British

expansion, to set up a trading centre, were the reasons for the establishment of Singapore. After 150 years Singapore has become an independent state with a flourishing multi-racial population. It is not the Malta of the East, the pawn in a colonial power game. Of the three motives given by Raffles for the establishment of Singapore only one remains valid, the development of trades of a commercial emporium. The other two, to destroy the power of a neighbouring government, and to expand as circumstances may require, are now considered dangerous and undesirable.

In the appraisal of Raffles' political philosophy both the negative and positive sides should be considered. From the point of view of the people of the region one of the few virtues of Raffles was his interest in learning. Many others are doubtful. An evaluation from this point of view is to be distinguished from an evaluation of Raffles' career as a colonial administrator. Given the colonial setting, Raffles was probably the best choice for anyone living in a British colony, but he was certainly not the best choice if the object was to increase the standard of humanity in this region. As a matter of fact Raffles had made colonial rule more oppressive because of his taxation policy. He was keen on introducing laissez-faire capitalism and a money economy in so far as it promoted British interests. He suggested the abolition of forced labour in Java and Sumatra only in the areas where he thought it was unprofitable. But in the Preanger Regencies of West Java he retained the system. He suggested the abolition of slavery only to replace it with something equally, if not more, oppressive: contract labour and debt bondage.

British writers, untrained in the social sciences, tend to consider the thought and action of Raffles in isolation of the entire historical configuration. They tend to judge Raffles primarily on what he and his widow claimed. They view Raffles as an enlightened despot or autocrat. They consider him as a person who had the welfare of the natives at heart. In their works attention is mostly focused on themes bearing direct interest on their affairs. Only in passing are the effects of Raffles' administration on native societies mentioned. The defects and ill effects of some of his actions are considered as well intended errors. Hence Bastin, a sober and dedicated scholar who has done more research than other historians or writers on Raffles could offer the following conclusion on Raffles:

> Raffles is best understood as conforming to a policy, no less pronounced in Dutch than in British colonial practice, of paternalism — of beneficient autocracy. He was not a pioneer of any modern system of native administration, although in Java he pointed the way to the idea of village government. His important contribution to the development of British and Dutch colonial policy was that he based his administrations upon humanitarian principles. He was not the first to do so, but neither was he the last. Less than a century after his death the principle of trusteeship was written into the Covenant of the League of Nations.[2]

Those who portray Raffles as a reformer and humanitarian on the whole have not taken the trouble to analyse what the terms mean. Both terms are loaded with value-judgements and unless carefully scrutinized would give rise to a false impression. A Dutch author, Ottow, called Raffles a "word-pedlar" ("woord-kramer").[3] His words expressing nice thoughts were profusely distributed in his writings. When we say that Raffles was a humanitarian reformer what do we mean by that? Let us analyse its meaning within the context of the time. Raffles' dominant motive was to advance British interests. The rest were subordinated to this central goal. He wanted to make the Malay Archipelago and the Dutch East Indies a market for British manufacture in India. He was ahead of his Dutch contemporaries in the sense that he conceived Western imperialism as a comprehensive effort of the European to transform the societies of others for their own benefit. He had what *wissensoziologie* ("the sociology of knowledge") calls the "total ideology" concept of imperialism. It is an all-embracing capitalist transformation dominated by the imperial power covering all the major aspects of life.

The essence of Raffles' ideology of imperialism is expressed in the following notes on the establishment of a Malay college in Singapore, 1819:

> By collecting the traditions of the country, and affording the means of instruction to all who visit our stations, we shall give an additional inducement to general intercourse; while the merchant will pursue his gain, the representative of our government will acquire a higher character and more general respect, by devoting a portion of his time to the diffusion of that knowledge and of those principles, which form the happiness and basis of all

civilized society. The native inhabitant who will be first attracted
by commerce, will imbibe a respect for our institutions, and
when he finds that some of these are destined exclusively for his
own benefit, while he applauds and respects the motive he will
not fail to profit by them. Our civil institutions and political
influence are calculated to increase the population and wealth
of these countries, and cultivation of mind seems alone wanting
to raise them to such a rank among the nations of the world as
their geographical situation and climate may admit. And shall
we, who have been so favoured among other nations, refuse to
encourage the growth of intellectual improvement, or rather
shall we not consider it one of our first duties to afford the means
of education to surrounding countries, and thus render our sta-
tions not only the seats of commerce but of literature and arts?
Will not our best inclinations and feelings be thus gratified, at the
same time that we are contributing to raise millions in the scale of
civilization? It may be observed, that in proportion as the people
are civilized, our intercourse with the islands will become more
general, more secure, and more advantageous; that the native
riches of the countries which they inhabit seem inexhaustible,
and that the eventual extent of our commerce with them must
consequently depend on the growth of intellectual improvement and the extension of moral principles.[4]

The general progress for the people of this area, as he himself
said, would make it more advantageous to the British. Being
civilized in Raffles' sense was to serve British mercantile capitalist interest. In actual life the actions and ideas of Raffles were
not the most humanitarian by an enlightened 19th-century
European standard. In 19th-century Europe there were people who opposed the enslavement of nations, which imperi-

alism was, and instead suggested as substitutes economic and cultural contacts. There were people who questioned the moral basis of imperialism, and would condemn what Raffles had done. Raffles was what Karl Marx would call a "civilization-monger".[5] His talk about reforming native society was part of the imperialist ideology, a justification for those measures which could serve the imperialist interest. Even naked force was given a respectable appearance. Here is an instance. In January 1813 Raffles approved of the efforts of Cornelius, a Dutch surveyor, in transmigrating colonists from Java to the Carimon Island, by force if necessary. All "suspect and less criminal persons", Chinese, Malays, and Javanese, were to be transported with their families. Raffles was however not in favour of forced recruitment of soldiers for Ceylon but approved forced transmigration to Banjarmasin and the Carimon Island. The respectable justification for this measure, in the style of an imperialist ideology, was the following:

> Other objects were indeed nearer to Raffles' heart than the recruitment of soldiers for Ceylon. He cherished a vision of the establishment throughout the Archipelago of British settlements, which would suppress piracy and radiate civilization. Since there was plenty of uncultivated land in Java, it was not easy to recruit voluntary Javanese colonists for such settlements.[6]

Again, in the imperialist ideology everything was given a noble motive so much so that the exponent or pioneer of imperialism, the empire-builder, always appeared under the garb of a humanitarian. The more forceful motive for the abolition of slavery, for instance, the aggressive and acquisitive passion for maximum gain, was rarely admitted by the self-professed humanitarian. The best instance is Raffles' attitude towards slavery. In the East Indies slavery among the local population was mild and incomparable to the West Indies and America. Benjamin Heyne, a surgeon and naturalist on the Madras establishment, who visited Sumatra in 1812, noted how mildly and kindly the slaves were treated in Benkulen, particularly by the local families. He made the following comparison:

> I cannot but mention here an observation which I have often heard made, that halfcaste Europeans and the Indians themselves are much better masters to their slaves and servants than Europeans: they are more attentive to their wants and comforts, which indeed are much the same as their own; they treat them, if not with familiarity, at least with greater placidity and indulgence; and in return are better served, and get servants who will adhere to them in all vicissitudes of life; whereas Europeans always complain of the rascality and ingratitude of all their Indian servants and followers, and are forsaken by them and robbed as soon as it suits their convenience.[7]

It was a sociological fact that much slave-labour was absorbed by the home. To create a free floating wage-earning plantation labour, it would be necessary to abolish slavery. Since the homes would not be in the position to pay wages in money, there would be more labour available for the British plantation.

Thus Raffles desired the abolition of slavery and forced

labour because it was more advantageous economically. According to Bastin it is difficult to say whether economic motives supersede the humanitarian ones in Raffles' thinking. Bastin cited the following words of Raffles:

> The time is past when the Company looked for her profits from the sale of a yard of broadcloth or a pound of nails: she now acts in a more extended sphere, and her principles have expanded with the growth of her empire. She now looks to the wealth and enterprize of those whom she governs, as the sure and only sources of her own financial prosperity.[8]

But the crucial factor in deciding what was good and humanitarian was at his own discretion. We have shown how Raffles thought it was for the good of the country to deport people by force to Banjarmasin and the Carimon Island. Similarly it was for the good of the country to have wages at subsistence level. A year after the establishment of Singapore, on August 20, 1820, Raffles wrote to the Duke of Somerset from Bencoolen (Benkulen), of his plan to grow sugar and manufacture sugar on the same principles as in the West Indies. He wrote with glowing enthusiasm on the advantages of Sumatra, two of which were land and labour. He said,

> For instance in an estate calculated to afford two hundred or two hundred and fifty tons of sugar annually, the kind alone would cost eight thousand or ten thousand pounds in Jamaica, while here it may be had for nothing. The negroes would there cost ten or twelve thousand pounds more, while here labourers may

be obtained on contract, or by the month, with a very moderate advance, at wages not higher than necessary for the subsistence.[9]

As apparent from the above, Raffles, then, was in favour of wages which would be no higher than was necessary for subsistence. As Wright noted, "In Batavia he continued the vain endeavour of the previous government to keep wages down by police measures to a rate which government departments in practice found it necessary to exceed, owing to the high prices and currency difficulties."[10] However, when it concerned the interest of British settlers, he was against a return not beyond bare subsistence level.[11] Here we see the familiar double standard of the ideologist of imperialism, for his people one standard of goodness, for another a different standard. In calling his principles humanitarian the standard used by British authors was their own colonial standard, not the universal standard. Raffles' system of administration was more reasonable than that of his predecessors in Bencoolen (Benkulen). But why Raffles and the British should be there at all to force the people to plant pepper and maintain the establishment was never questioned! What is humanitarian in that? The most dominant single passion in the personality of Raffles was territorial conquest and the acquisition of wealth for the glory of England. All that stood in the way of the expansion were to be overthrown. Once dominated, the subject people were to be changed and made to conform to what Raffles thought was profitable to the British in the first place. His entire conduct was not dominated by a broad love for humanity as one would find in a Godwin or Tolstoy, but by the fanatical glorification of the English at the expense of other nationalities. By an enlightened 19th-century standard his general ethical and intellectual outlook was parochial and superficial. The historian of civilization would consider the philosophy of Raffles as an example of the parochial nationalism which was prevalent during the period of the nation states in Europe.

Raffles belonged to the generation of parochial nationalists which modern European thought has condemned as dangerous, unsound and decisive. The passion to glorify the English at the expense of other nations was strong, not only in Raffles, but also in his family circle, as is apparent from the letters of his cousin Thomas Raffles. Thomas Raffles visited Paris in the summer of 1817. After having been in France for some time, he noted an officer he met whose face was the first French face that pleased him.[12] The Reverend Thomas Raffles, friend and cousin of Raffles, saw even in English prostitution a superior form. He said to Raffles:

> In our own metropolis alas, there is enough vice, and crimes are perpetrated of the deepest die. But then, vice is recognized as vice, and shunned and abhorred by virtue. It keeps its own form, uses its own language, and preserves its own limits. But here, vice has the language and form of virtue — walks hand in hand with virtue — is adorned with the same attire — admitted into the same society — occupies the same seat — and, I had almost said, reposes on the same couch. She is to be found in the shops of the respectable tradesmen, in forms that in London would be

shrouded with the greatest secrecy, or, if discovered, brand the
vendor with deserved infamy — but here, the softer sex become
the ministers of lust, by exposing them to such as choose to purchase, and that too with unblushing countenance, as if they were
the simplest of articles of lawful commerce — the fine arts have
lent their aid to decorate and adorn the monster, and to give a
soft and classic air to her most disgusting expressions — while
the brilliant genius and the exuberant imagination of the author,
have invested it as with dazzling gems and a gorgeous robe.[13]

The superiority of the English virtue was not that it did not
repose in the same couch with vice but that it did it quietly
without any effort to justify it. The Reverend Thomas Raffles
found the English people the happiest, the English towns and
cities the most prosperous, in their passage through the continent it became the duty of the English to leave "favourable
traces of British piety, or British morals, or even British honesty."[14]

The political philosophy of Raffles is the ideology of imperialism par excellence. Ethical principles are subordinated to
economic and political motives. It employs a respectable
vocabulary to express motives which may not otherwise seem
dignified. Hence in advocating despotism Raffles claimed to
be the "true and steady friend of national freedom".[15] In
destroying the social institutions of weaker societies the imperialists claimed they were reforming those societies. In com-
pelling people to cultivate cash crops the imperialists claimed
to be encouraging the acquisitive spirit to earn more. In keeping wages down they claimed to develop prosperity. In abol-

ishing slavery and debt bondage they introduced contract labour and slavery in the more rigorous form of a debt bondage. In Bencoolen (Benkulen) Raffles introduced his new system of labour and abolished the traditional debt slavery. In exchange he allowed a maximum of 10 years for debt bondage no matter what the amount was. Ten rupiahs were considered the wage of one year's labour. Anything exceeding 100 rupiahs debt was to be redeemed by not more than 10 years labour. On paper this sounds like an improvement on the existing situation. But he also involved the long arms of the law. Debtors were forbidden to leave their masters. If their work was not satisfactory they were to be punished at the discretion of the local courts. All labour contracts were to be registered at the magistrate's office.[16] Consequently Raffles' new regulations gave more power to the masters. Though the bondage was limited to 10 years, the freedom to resist any oppression within this period was curtailed, for the authority had become involved in keeping the slave to his master.

Judging by the mild and reasonable condition of employment in the homes of the masters, and bearing in mind that those bound in debt servitude were in the position to desert their masters if they were improperly treated, the regulations of Raffles made the system more severe. They could lead to the creation of unemployment the moment the homes could no more absorb debt labour. Unemployment would create cheap labour and this would be favourable to British interests in Bencoolen (Benkulen). As things stand now, strictly speaking we are not in a position to qualify the so called "reforms" of

Raffles as good or bad. There has never been any sociological investigation made. However the arguments adduced against his so-called "reforms" in Java and Sumatra incline more to the negative side. On paper many things can be presented as sound and human. But in reality if we look into the motives and the effects of certain measures they may appear rather ugly.

In Raffles' time there were here and there abuses and cruelties committed against the slaves. These were mainly by those dealing with the commercial exports of slaves, by Europeans and native dealers. Such instances were often cited by Raffles to excuse his acquisition of new territories for the East India Company, The island of Nias was such an instance. The island was agriculturally rich, the inhabitants industrious, geographically well situated. The apology for the acquisition of Nias was to end the slave trade. However Raffles himself admitted it was economically advantageous to the Company. By converting the system into his form of debt bondage, he restricted the export of the labour force from the British area of interest. Economic gains dominated his acquisition of Nias. If Raffles was the humanitarian his admirers thought he was, why was he silent on the evils and injustice of his own society? He had never protested against the shortcomings of his own society while he loved to gloat on the defects of Southeast Asian societies, particularly those that were to become the object of his imperial expansion. During the time of Raffles England was under a social system so oppressive to the poor that it horrified thinkers and reformers of the period.

Examine, for instance, the condition of the working class between 1750 and 1850 in England. The handloom weavers laboured fourteen hours and upward daily earning from five to seven shillings a week. They were ill-fed, ill-clothed, half-sheltered and ignorant, working in closed damp cellars, or crowded ill-ventilated workshops. They became demoralized and reckless so much so that their life could be portrayed as savage. To reduce wages further, a system of fines was introduced by employers. If a worker in a spinning factory fell ill and could not find a replacement in time, the cost of the steam unused owing to his absence was deducted from his pay. This could be as much as half his weekly wage.

Another device invented by employers so as to gain further profit by exploiting the workers was making it compulsory for workers to buy at company controlled stores at prices far above normal. Then there was the notorious adulteration of food. Loaves of bread were doctored with alum to increase the size, milk was diluted, and butter was often rancid and contained up to 33% water. One can go on endlessly describing the inhuman conditions and exploitation of the poor in England during Raffles' time. It was one of the worst periods in English history. Even children were exploited.

One can even say that for some time child labour formed the basis of the factory system. Certain kinds of work, especially in the textile industries, were done only by children; and according to opinion among the ruling classes this was perfectly right. William Pitt, Prime Minister around the turn of the century, proposed in his Poor Law Bill that children should start work at the age of five; and since the work required only a low mental equipment, a Lancashire mill owner readily agreed to take one idiot with every twenty children furnished him by a London parish. In the factories and mines the children worked for twelve or even more hours. Often they slept in the factories or fell asleep beside the machines during their working hours; innumerable accidents happened in this way.[18]

While Raffles, then sixteen years old, was working as a clerk in the East India Company, he could have read the following note in *The Times* of July 22, 1797:

> The increasing value of the fair sex is regarded by many writers as the certain index of a growing civilization. Smithfield may for this reason claim to be a contributor to particular progress in finesse, for in the market the price was again raised from one half a guinea to three-and-one half.[18]

The above refers to the sale of women, wives by their husbands. While Raffles was trying to "reform" Javanese society, an event took place in England which should be of interest to a civilization-monger like Raffles.

In 1814 Henry Cook of Effingham, Surrey, was forced under the bastardy laws to marry a woman of Slinfold, Sussex, and six months after the marriage she and her child were removed to the Effingham workhouse. The governor there, having contracted to maintain all the poor for the specific sum of £210, complained of the new arrivals, whereupon the parish officer to Effingham prevailed on Cook to sell his wife.

The master of the workhouse, Chippen, was directed to take the woman to Croydon market and there, on June 17, 1815, she was sold to John Earl for the sum of one shilling which had been given to Earl for the purchase.[20]

In 1823, a year before Raffles finally went home for the last time, a number of wives were sold by their husbands. *The History Teachers' Miscellany* for May 1925, contains an article by H. W. V. Temperley entitled, "Sale of Wives in England in 1823". R. W. Emerson, a benevolent critic of England said in 1856, in his *English Traits*, that "the right of the husband to sell his wife has been retained down to our times".[21]

Raffles and other ideologists of empire-building did not raise a single word of protest against the social injustice and barbarism in their own society, unlike men such as William Godwin, Robert Owen, William Cobbet, Richard Cobden, and a host of others. Thus measured by the British standard of humanitarian consciousness prevailing in his time. Raffles was far below the mark. He was on the side of the establishment, on the side of the expansionist, the war-monger, the capitalist, and was what Cobden would call an advocate of knockdown diplomacy. The essence of this diplomacy, when described in terms of individual merchant behaviour, "was, to waylay their customers, whom they first knocked down and disabled, and afterwards dragged into their stores and compelled to purchase whatever articles they chose to offer, at such prices as they chose to ask".[22]

However if we judge Raffles within the context of British domination in particular areas, there would be a great deal of difference between him and an East India Company servant such as Resident Parr of Benkulen. In comparison with other colonial careerists Raffles was definitely a more enlightened person. But compared with the wider circle of thinkers and reformers, he was philosophically and ethically a dwarf, not a giant like Tolstoy, Robert Owen, and other great humanitarian reformers. Raffles was just one of the hundreds of enthusiastic pioneers of empire building moved by the lust for gain. To rank him as a humanitarian reformer is to abuse the use of the term, particularly after what we have known of the man. Another aspect of Raffles' life, his alleged corruption in Java, has not been treated here. It requires a special treatment and it only reinforces the conclusion of this book.

In conclusion, we may summarize our view on Raffles as follows. For the following reasons he was not a humanitarian reformer as his admirers made him out to be: (a) A humanitarian reformer is guided by principles of humanity to which his views and actions are subordinated irrespective of their being advantageous or not to the interest of his group. (b) A humanitarian reformer usually possesses a broad and tolerant outlook on other communities and nations. He does not scorn the religion and culture of other people. He does not naively preach the superiority of his own nation in a manner that requires the degradation of other nations. (c) A humanitarian reformer is in the first place concerned with the injustice within his own society. He does not direct his criticism only towards alien societies. (d) A humanitarian reformer does not consider it his mission in life to build an empire at the cost of other nations.

(e) A humanitarian reformer does not spend the best years of his life scheming and intriguing as Raffles did.

It is hoped that the portrayal of Raffles' thoughts and actions in this book will be considered as an attempt to correct the persistent historical canonization of Raffles as a lovable and gentle personality surrounded by jealous competitors, as an heroic reformer who wanted to bring peace and progress to the people of the area in which he operated. It is the British colonial historians more than any other group who have been responsible in large for the historical canonization of this man. There is a great need to review the entire historical writing in this region with a view to accomplish a deeper, more meaningful and objective portrayal of history.

Notes to the Text

CHAPTER 1

[1] An exception should be made of John Bastin's work, *The Native Policies of Sir Stamford Raffles in Java and Sumatra,* Oxford University Press, London 1957.

[2] See Emily Hahn, *Raffles of Singapore,* Doubleday, New York 1946. It is a case in point. It is a one-sided biography of Raffles. It ignores the well-known Dutch accusation that Raffles instigated the Massacre of Palembang on September 14, 1811. Her treatment of this episode is unreliable. The selection of data is aimed at building up Raffles as a progressive statesman. Nothing of the schemer is discussed.

[3] Letter to Thomas Murdoch, October 9, 1820 (Bencoolen) quoted in S. Raffles, *Memoir of the Life and Public Services of Sir Thomas Stamford Raffles* (by his widow), John Duncan, London 1835, Vol. II, pp. 160-2.

[4] Letter to the Duchess of Somerset, June 12, 1821, *Memoir...*, Vol. II, p. 193.

[5] M. L. van Deventer, *Het Nederlandsch Gezag over Java en Onderhoorigheden sedert 1811,* Martinus Nijhoff, The Hague 1891, p. 32.

[6] *Memoir...*, Vol. II, p. 141.

[7] *Memoir...*, Vol. II, pp. 165-66. See letter to Thomas Murdoch.

[8] The role of the British here was to help in the establishment of peace and stability, to create a powerful and active nation, which without becoming formidable to the British would be formidable to any other nation. Letter to Lord Minto (Malacca), June 10, 1811. See *Memoir...*, Vol. I, p. 67. The increase of security would develop the population and wealth and these, in turn, would increase the consumption of opium, piece-goods, and other Indian commodities which the British could supply. *Memoir...*, Vol. I, p. 66.

[9] The instance was Sungai Lamo in Sumatra: "Had it been an object with the British government, the undisputed sovereignty of the country might doubtless have been obtained, but as every useful purpose is answered by our administering the country in the name of the Pangeran, I have thought this arrangement preferable." *Sumatra Factory Records,* Vol. 47, July 4, 1818, India Office Library, London. See J. Bastin, *The British in West Sumatra*

(1685-1825), University of Malaya Press, Kuala Lumpur 1965.

[10] See Raffles' letter to the Committee of the British and Foreign Bible Society, February 1825. *Memoir...*, Vol. II, pp. 351–61.

[11] *Memoir...*, Vol. II, p. 355.

[12] Letter to the Duke of Somerset, Bencoolen, August 20, 1820, *Memoir...*, Vol. II, p. 151.

[13] He said, "For instance, in an estate calculated to afford two hundred or two hundred and fifty tons of sugar annually, the land alone would cost eight thousand or ten thousand pounds in Jamaica, while here it may be had for nothing. The negroes there cost ten or twelve thousand pound more, while here labourers may be obtained on contract, or by the month with a very moderate advance, at wages not higher than necessary for their subsistence." *Memoir...*, Vol. II, pp. 147–8.

CHAPTER 2

[1] J. C. Baud, "Palembang in 1811 en 1812", *BTLV*, Vol. I, No. 1, 1852.

[2] See J. Bastin, *The Native Policies of Sir Stamford Raffles in Java and Sumatra.* Not one reference was made to Raffles' relation with Palembang and the entire episode, despite the fact that the subsequent activity of Raffles in Sumatra after 1816, with reference to the British acquisition of Banka and the reaction it elicited from the Dutch

Government, was a result of Raffles' treaty with Palembang. If there was any great dispute which had strained Dutch-British relations after 1816 during Raffles' presence in Sumatra, it was Banka.

I fail to understand Bastin's omission of Raffles' activity concerning Palembang and Banka. He did, however, discuss this in a subsequent publication years later. Bastin's assessment of Raffles as an humanitarian autocrat is biased in a refined sense. His study was too document-centred and was not balanced by actual happenings in Java and Sumatra with reference to Raffles' concept of humanitarian government. For instance, while Raffles' views on the abolition of slavery were discussed in detail, his ruthless policy of employing convict-labour imported from abroad (with iron chains on their ankles), and the notorious Banjarmasin Affair and Raffles' forced deportation of convicts and suspected criminals to the Celebes, were omitted.

[3] Emily Hahn, *Raffles of Singapore,* p. 165. Her errors cannot be excused considering the fact that the subject has been much discussed, and she was aware of the sources, which appears in her bibliography to the above title.

[4] D. Macdonald, *A Narrative of the Early Life and Service,* 3rd edn Weymouth n.d. The date is not mentioned on the third edition, the first is presumably 1830. See pp. 84-85, and Appendix C, Raffles' letter of instruction. Macdonald referred to the Massacre and his motive to

clear Raffles from any responsibility, "as in after times it was basely attempted to connect the name of Sir Stamford Raffles with the sanguinary catastrophe which ensued", p. 85.

[5] Major M. H. Court, *An Exposition of the Relations of the British Government with the Sultan and State of Palembang,* Black-Allen, London 1821, see pp. 4–7.

[6] P. H. van der Kemp, *Oost Indisch Herstel in 1816,* Martinus Nijhoff, The Hague 1911, p. 340 note 2.

[7] C. E. Wurtzburg, "Raffles and the Massacre of Palembang", *JMBRAS,* Vol. XXII, Pt 1, 1949.

[8] W. Ph. Coolhaas, "Baud on Raffles", *JMBRAS,* Vol. XXIV, pt 1, 1951.

9 J. J. van Klaveren, *The Dutch Colonial System in the East Indies,* Rotterdam n.d., p. 87.

[10] Raffles' instruction in Macdonald, *A Narrative...,* Appendix C.

[11] Reproduced by Baud, "Palembang in 1811 en 1812", *BTLV,* Vol. I, No. 1, 1853, Appendix S, p. 27.

[12] Baud's transliteration is the following: "Iinie njang kedoea, miesti sobat beta boeang, abieskan sekali kalie; segala orang olanda. — den Residentnja. Den segala Orang njang die bauwa hoekoen Olanda; mana njang doedoek sekarang inie die dalam negrie Plembang, yan-gan kasie tiengal lagie." "Palembang in 1811 en 1812", *BTLV,* No. 1, 1852, p. 24. As the letter was definitely in Jawi, the spelling and the punctuation need not be the

same as those rendered in Baud's article. For convenience I have used the present spelling and in no way does it affect the translation as the sentence is unambiguous. The controversial part is the phrase "boeang, abieskan sekali kalie", "throw away", "finish entirely".

[13] C. E. Wurtzburg, "Raffles and the Massacre of Palembang", *JMBRAS,* Vol. XXII, Pt 1, 1949, p. 52.

[14] Baud, "Palembang in 1811 en 1812", *BTLV,* Vol. I, No. 1, 1852, pp. 21-2. The text is the following: "maka inie beta ada banjag tjienta sama sahabat beta, maoe menjadie sahabat njang baee dengan bersie ati, njang jangan die blakang arie ber sahabat sama laeen orang — maka itoe orang Olanda apa goena sobat beta betoelkan kasie tiengal dalam negrie Plembang, kerna orang Olanda ada banjag jahat — dia maoe bekeen satoe jalan — njang jahat joega, sama sahabat beta, sebab itoe beta ada banjag soesa ati darie sahabat beta trada jadie, sahabat sama Companie Jngries — Dan kaloe sahabat beta ada soeka menjadie sahabat njang betoel sama Companie Jngries miesti sahabat beta tentoekan sekalie kalie: lagie minta balas soeraat inie — dan soerat njang dole dengan begitoe lekas — lagie dengan sagala bietjara bitjaranja orang Olanda dengan sobat beta, lagie beta mienta satoe orang Wachil pada sobat beta — biar datang kepada beta." Dated 17 Zulkaidah 1224 A.H.

[15] Wurtzburg, "Raffles and the Massacre of Palembang", *JMBRAS,* Vol. XXII, Pt 1, 1949, p. 51.

[16] "Bicharanya" here may mean "talks", "promises", or

even "concluded agreements". Raffles wanted to know them as well.

[17] He criticized Baud without considering all his arguments as some appeared in parts of the Dutch text not translated into English for Wurtzburg's use. The greater part of Baud's article was translated and it was on this that Wurtzburg based his attack on Baud. Without mastering Dutch and Malay, Wurtzburg was bold enough to explain Raffles' position in connection with the Massacre of Palembang.

[18] In the records both Tunku Radin Mohammed and Tunku Sharif Mohammed are used in reference to the one person as are Syed Abu Bakar and Syed Abu Bakar bin Hussein Rum for the other of Raffles' agents.

[19] As indicated in the letter Raffles was familiar with the Malacca Report on the Massacre. This letter also mentioned the attempt to forge and seal false reports by the Sultan. See S. Raffles, *Memoir...*, Vol. I, pp. 157–8.

[20] See *Asiatic Journal,* March 1819, p. 319 where the English version of the treaty is given.

[21] For a detailed account see Court, *An Exposition...*, Badruddin was popular with the people and posed a continuous threat to the British–created Sultan.

[22] *Memoir...*, Vol. I, p. 173.

[23] Court, *An Exposition...*, p. 5.

[24] J. Bastin (ed.), *The Journal of Thomas Otto Travers —*

1813-1820, Memoirs of the Raffles Museum, No. 4, May 1957, Singapore 1960.

[25] Quoted by Bastin in "Palembang in 1811 and 1812", *BTLV,* Vol. 110, 1954, p. 78. The earlier part is in Vol. 109, 1953; the primary source is "Case of Major Robison — late Resident of Palembang and the island of Banca, Calcutta, 25 Jan. 1814" in *Bengal Civil Colonial Consultations,* Range 167. Vol. 53, Consultations of April 28, 1814, Pt III.

[26] "Palembang in 1811 and 1812", *BTLV,* Vol. 110, 1954, p. 78.

[27] Levyssohn Norman, *De Britsche Heerschappij over Java en Onderhoorigheden (1811-1816),* Belinfante, 'S-Gravenhage 1857, p. 87. The translation is mine.

[28] W. Ph. Coolhaas, "Baud on Raffles", *JMBRAS,* Vol. XXIV, Pt 1, 1951, p. 119.

[29] Coolhaas, "Baud on Raffles", *JMBRAS,* Vol. XXIV, Pt 1, 1951, p. 120.

[30] P. J. Veth, *Java,* Vol. 2, Bohn, Haarlem 1968, p. 296, notes, 1, 2. Here Veth stated that he was wrong in considering Raffles incapable of murder. After reading Baud's work and some others, he believed that Raffles was guilty. Of Raffles' character Veth said, "The character of Raffles was not above blame. He belonged to those Englishmen who were British in the first place and human in the second place, and thereby showed in many instances that he was capable of trampling under his feet the demands of

humanity, prudence and justice, where it served British interests." p. 295. The translation is mine.

[31] Bastin, "Palembang in 1811 and 1812", *BTLV*, Vol. 110, 1954, p 80

[32] To illustrate this with an instance, a man may be guilty in both the following circumstances: (a) Set his house on fire to burn his wife (attitude expressed in action, though not necessarily in words, the motive being established by circumstantial evidences), (b) House on fire and allow his wife to be burned by not rescuing her (attitude expressed in inaction).

[33] Macdonald, *A Narrative...*, p. 84: Raffles' instruction to Macdonald was verbal.

[34] *Raffles Collection,* Vol. IV, No. 12. See also Bastin, "Palembang in 1811 and 1812", *BTLV,* Vol. 110, 1954, p. 84.

[35] He blamed Raffles for it. Raffles' inflammatory proclamations were circulated amongst the people of Sungsang at the mouth of Palembang River. See his statement as quoted by Robison in Bastin, "Palembang in 1811 and 1812", *BTLV,* Vol. 110, 1954, p. 77.

[36] *Memoir...*, *Vol. I, p. 46.*

[37] See Baud, "Palembang in 1811 en 1812", *BTLV,* No. 1, 1852, pp. 16–17, and Wurtzburg, "Raffles and the Massacre of Palembang", *JMBRAS,* Vol. XXII, Pt 1, 1949, p. 46 for the English translation.

[38] Bastin noted the dates Raffles received the reports,

"Palembang in 1811 and 1812", *BTLV,* Vol. 110, 1954, p. 69.

[39] Letters of Raffles to Minto, March 7, 1812, *Memoir...,* Vol. I, pp. 155-72. No mention was made of the treaty with Badruddin. The entire letter is a distorted account of the British relation with Palembang.

[40] See pp. 55-58, this book, for text and translation.

[41] See Bastin, p. 76, Robison's letter to Raffles, July 28, 1813, *Java Factory Records,* "Palembang in 1811 and 1812", *BTLV,* Vol. 110, 1954, Vol. 37.

[42] Baud, "Palembang in 1811 en 1812", *BTLV,* Vol. I, No. 1, 1853, p. 30. The preceding Romanized text and the English translation are mine from an original Jawi version found in *Raffles Collection,* Vol. IV, No. 127, University of Singapore Library (Microfilms).

[43] P. H. van der Kemp, *Het Nederlandsch-Indisch Bestuur in het Midden van 1817*, Martinus Nijhoff, The Hague, 1915. See Goldberg's letter, August 1, 1817, pp. 366-70.

[44] According to my reconstructed chronology, from the report, the date should be September 23, 1811.

[45] Baud, "Palembang in 1811 en 1812", *BTLV,* No. 1, 1852, pp. 38-40.

[46] As noted earlier, this was also suggested by Robison. He doubted the reliability of the two agents. The Range ran Ratu was apparently never employed for public business by the Sultan according to Robison. See Bastin,

"Palembang in 1811 and 1812", *BTLV,* Vol. 110, 1954, p. 76.

[47] Baud, "Palembang in 1811 en 1812", *BTLV,* Vol. I, No. 1, 1853, Appendix 3, p. 24.

[48] Bastin, "Palembang in 1811 and 1812", *BTLV,* Vol. 109, 1953, pp. 301–2.

CHAPTER 3

[1] S. Raffles, *Memoir*…, Vol. 1, pp. 258–9, letter to Hugh Inglis, February 13, 1814.

[2] *Memoir*…, Vol. I, pp. 80–1, letter to Lord Minto (Malacca), June 10, 1811.

[3] *Memoir*…, Vol. I, p. 82. The passage was endorsed and quoted by Raffles from the report of the counsellors of Batavia.

[4] *Memoir*…, Vol. I, pp. 82–3.

[5] *Memoir*…, Vol. I, pp. 83–4.

[6] *Memoir*…, Vol. I, p. 94.

[7] *Memoir*…, Vol. I, p. 104.

[8] *Memoir*…, Vol. I, pp. 85–6.

[9] *Memoir*…, Vol. I, p. 86. The first sentence in the quotation is grammatically odd.

[10] *Memoir*…, Vol. I, p. 107.

[11] S. Raffles, *Memoir*…, Vol. II, pp. 94–5. See also his letter to the Duchess of Somerset, February 12, 1820.

[12] *Memoir*…, Vol. II, p. 95.

[13] Abdullah bin Abdul Kadir Munshi, *Hikayat Abdullah,* R. A. Datoek Besar and R. Roelvink (eds), Penerbit Djambatan, Djakarta, 1953, p. 220.

[14] Lt. Kolonel Nahuijs, *Brieven over Bencoolen, Padang, het Rijk van Menangkabau, Rhiauw, Sincapoera en Poelo Penang*, Hollingerus Pijpers, Breda MDCCCXXVI, p. 244.

CHAPTER 4

[1] J. Hageman, "Geschiedkundige Aanteekeningen Omtrent Zuidelijk Borneo", TNI, Vol. 23, No. 4, 1861, p. 226.

[2] J. C. Baud, "De Bandjarmasinsche Afschuwelijkheid", *BTLV,* Vol. VII, No. 3, 1860, Appendix I, p. 17, letter of James Simpson to W. Boggie.

[3] J. C. Baud, "Palembang in 1811 en 1812", *BTLV,* Vol. VII, No. I, 1853, p. 9.

[4] T. S. Raffles, "Discourse delivered at a meeting of the Society on the 23rd April 1813", *Transaction of the Batavian Society of Arts and Science,* Vol. VII, Batavia 1814, p. 27.

[5] Between 1812 and 1816 the expenditure of the colony was 649,685 Dutch rupiahs while the income was 92,915. The loss in about 4 years was thus 556,770 Dutch rupiahs. See the accountant's report in Baud, "De Bandjarmanische Afschuwelijkheid", *BTLV,* Vol. VII, No. 3, 1860, p. 25.

[6] See the report of J. van Boeckholtz, the Dutch Commissioner sent to inquire into Banjarmasin and to arrange for the restitution of Dutch rule in Indonesia, *TNI,* Vol. 23, Pt 6, 1861, pp. 358–64.

[7] C. Assey, Secretary to Government, *Circular No. 160, to Lieut. Jourdan, Resident Passeroang,* April 25, 1815, in Baud, "De Bandjarmasinsche Afschuwelijkheid", *BTLV,* Vol. VII, No. 3, 1860, p. 20.

[8] "De Bandjarmasinsche Afschuwelijkheid", Baud, *BTLV,* Vol. VII, No. 3, 1860, p. 11.

[9] "De Bandjarmasinsche Afschuwelijkheid", Baud, *BTLV,* Vol. VII, No. 3, 1860, p. 22.

[10] See his report in Baud, "De Bandjarmasinsche Afschuwelijkheid", *BTLV,* Vol. VII, No. 3, 1860, p. 24. The period was 1812 to April 1816.

[11] Hare continued his despotic and colonizing adventures in the Cocos-Keeling Islands. See C. A. Gibson-Hill, (ed.), "Documents relating to John Clunies Ross, Alexander Hare and the Establishment of the Colony on the Cocos-Keeling islands", *JMBRAS,* Vol. XXV, Pts 4 and 5, December 1952.

CHAPTER 5

[1] S. Raffles, *Memoir…,* Vol. II, pp. 18–19.

[2] J. Bastin, *The Native Policies of Sir Stamford Raffles in*

Java and Sumatra, Oxford University Press, London 1957, pp. 141-2.

[3] J. J. van Klaveren, *The Dutch Colonial System in the East Indies,* n.p., Rotterdam 1953, p. 92.

[4] S. Raffles, *Memoir of the Life and Public Services of Sir Thomas Stamford Raffles,* John Murray, London 1830, Appendix, pp. 31-2.

[5] Karl Marx and F. Engels, *On Colonialism,* Foreign Language Publishing House, Moscow n.d., p. 127.

[6] H. R. C. Wright, "The Freedom of Labour under Raffles' Administration in Java (1811-1816)", *JMBRAS,* Vol. XXVI, Pt 1, 1953, p. 108.

[7] See his *Tracts* in J. Bastin, (ed.), *The British in West Sumatra 1685-1825,* University of Malaya Press, Kuala Lumpur 1965, p. 143.

[8] S. Raffles, *Memoir...,* p. 22, See J. Bastin, *The Native Policies of Sir Stamford Raffles in Java and Sumatra,* p. 139.

[9] S. Raffles, *Memoir...,* Vol. II, pp. 147-8.

[10] H. R. C. Wright, *East-Indian Economic Problems of the Age of Cornwallis and Raffles,* Luzac, London 1961, p. 104.

[11] S. Raffles, *Memoir...,* Vol. II, p. 149.

[12] Thomas Raffles, *Letters during a Tour through Some Parts of France, Savoy, Switzerland, Germany, And the Netherlands in the Summer of 1817,* n.p., Liverpool 1818, p. 107.

[13] *Letters...,* pp 72-3.

[14] *Letters...,* p. 121.

[15] *Memoir...*, Vol. II, p. 167.

[16] For source reference, see J. Bastin, *The Native Policies of Sir Stamford Raffles in Java and Sumatra,* p. 122.

[17] See P. H. van der Kemp, "Raffles Betrekkingen met Nias in 1820-1821", *BTLV,* Vol. 52, Pt 8, 1901, pp. 11-12.

[18] See J. Kuczynski, "A Short History of Labour under Industrial Capitalism" in *Great Britain 1750 to the Present Day,* Muller, London 1947, Vol. I, Pt 1, pp. 24-5.

[19] Viola Klein, *The Feminine Character,* Routledge and Kegan Paul, London 1946, p. 7.

[20] Viola Klein, *The Feminine Character,* pp. 7-8, quoted from Ivy Pinchbeck, *Women Workers and the Industrial Revolution,* Routledge and Kegan Paul, London 1930, p. 83.

[21] Viola Klein, *The Feminine Character,* p. 8.

[22] Quoted in A. P. Thorton, *Doctrines of Imperialism,* pp. 116-17, John Wiley and Sons Inc., New York 1965, pp. 116-17, from Richard Cobden, *Political Writings,* Vol. II, p. 221.

Bibliography

Alatas, Syed Hussein

"Archeology, History, and the Social Sciences", *Federation Museums Journal*, Kuala Lumpur, 1964.

"Reconstructions of Malaysian History", *Revue du Sudest Asiatique*, No. 3, Bruxelles 1962.

"Theoretical Aspects of Southeast Asian History", *Asian Studies*, Vol. II, No. 2, 1964, Manila.

Bastin, J.

The British in West Sumatra (1685-1825), University of Malaya Press, Kuala Lumpur, 1965. A selection of documents with notes and introduction.

(ed.), *The Journal of Thomas Otto Travers 1813-1820*, Memoirs of the Raffles Museum, No. 4, May 1957, Singapore 1960.

The Native Policies of Sir Stamford Raffles in Java and Sumatra, Oxford University Press, London 1957.

"Palembang in 1811 and 1812", *BTLV*, Vol. 109 (1953), Vol. 110 (1954).

"Raffles and British Policy in the Indian Archipelago, 1811–1816", *JMBRAS*, Vol XXVII, Pt 1, 1954.

"Raffles' Ideas on the Land Rent System in Java," *Verhandlingen Kon. Inst., Taal, Land en Volkenkunde*, deel IX, 1954.

"Sir Stamford Raffles and John Crawford's Ideas of Colonising the Malay Archipelago", *JMBRAS*, Vol. XXVI, Pt 1, 1953.

Baud, J. C.

"De Bandjarmasinsche Afschuwelijkheid", *BTLV*, Vol. VII, No. 3, 1860.

"Palembang in 1811 on 1812", *BTLV*, No. 1, 1852.

Boulger, D. C.

The Life of Sir Stamford Raffles, Horace Marshall, London 1899.

Cobden, Richard

Political Writings, Vol. II, John Wiley and Sons Inc., New York 1965.

Collis, Maurice

Raffles, Faber and Faber, London 1966.

Coolhaas, W. Ph.

"Baud on Raffles", *JMBRAS*, Vol. XXIV, Pt 1, 1951.

Coupland, R.

Raffles of Singapore, Collins, London 1946.

Court, M. H.

An Exposition of the Relations of the British Government with the Sultan of Palembang and the Designs of the Netherlands Government upon that Country, Black-Allen, London 1821.

Crawford, John

"*The History of Java*", *Edinburgh Review*, March 1819. This is a review of Sir Stamford Raffles' book.

Day, Clive

The Dutch in Java, Oxford University Press, London 1966.

van Deventer, M. L.

Het Nederlandsch Gezag over Java en Onderhoorigheden sedert 1811, Martinus Nijhoff, The Hague 1891.

Egerton, H. E.

Sir Stamford Raffles, Fisher Unwin, London 1946.

Freeman-Grenville, G. S. P.

The Muslim and Christian Calendars, Oxford University Press, London 1963.

Furnivall, J. S.

Netherlands India, Macmillan, New York 1944.

Gibson-Hill, C. A. (ed.)

"Documents Relating to John Clunies Ross, Alexander Hare and the Establishment of the Colony on the Cocos-Keeling Islands", *JMBRAS*, Vol. XXV, Pts 4-5, December 1952.

Godwin, William

An Enquiry Concerning Political Justice and Its Influence on

General Virtue and Happiness, R. A. Preston (ed.), Volumes 1 and 2, A. Knopf, New York 1936.

de Haan, F.

"Personalia der Periode van het Engelsch Bestuur over Java 1811–1816", *BTLV*, Vol. 92, Pt 4, 1935.

"Priangan", *Bataviaasch Genootschap van Kunsten en Wetenschappen*, Volumes 1–4, Batavia 1910–1912.

Hahn, Emily

Raffles of Singapore, Douhleday, New York 1946.

Hageman, J.

"Geschiedkundige Aanteekeningcn Omtrent Zuidelijk Borneo", *TNI*, Vol. 23, No. 4, 1861.

Hobson, J. A.

Imperialism, Allen and Unwin, London 1938.

Hough, G. G.

"The Educational Policy of Sir Stamford Raffles", *JMBRAS*, Vol. XI, Pt 2, 1933.

Hughes, J. C.

Kings of the Cocos, Methuen, London 1950.

de Kat Angelino, A. D. A.

Colonial Policy, Volumes 1 and 2, transl. G. J. Renier, Martinus Nijhoff, The Hague 1931.

van der Kemp, P. H.

"De Singapoorsche Papieroorlog", *BTLV*, Vol. 49, Pt 5, 1898.

"Fendall's en Raffles' Opvattingen in het Algemeen omtrent het Londonsch Tractaat van 12 Augustus

1814", *BTLV*, Vol. 47, Pt 3, 1897.

"Het Afbreken van Onze Bettrekinggen met Bandjermasin onder Daendels en de Herstelling van het Nederlansch Gezag aldaar op de 1 Januari 1817", *BTLV*, Vol. 49, Pt 5, 1898.

Het Nederlandsch-Indisch Bestuur in het Midden van 1817, Martinus Nijhoff, The Hague 1915.

Oost-Indisch Herstel in 1816, Martinus Nijhoff, The Hague 1911.

"Raffles' Bettrekkingen met Nias in 1820–1821", *BTLV*, Vol. 52, Pt 8, 1901.

Sumatra in 1818, Martinus Nijhoff, The Hague 1920.

van Klaveren, J. J.

The Dutch Colonial System in The East Indies, n.p., Rotterdam [1953].

Kloosterboer, W.

Involuntary Labour since the Abolition of Slavery, Brill, Leiden 1960.

Koebner, R. and Schmidt, H. D.

Imperialism, Cambridge University Press, London 1964.

Kohn, Hans

Prophets and People, Macmillan, New York 1952.

Kuczynski, J.

"A Short History of Labour Conditions Under Industrial Capitalism" in *Great Britain 1750 to the Present Day*, Vol. 1, Pt 1, F. Muller, London 1947.

van Leur, J. C.

  Indonesian Trade and Society, van Hoeve, The Hague
  1955.

Levyssohn Norman, H. D.

  *De Britsche Heerschappij over Java en Onderhoorigheden
  (1811-1916)*, Belinfante, 'S-Gravenhage 1857.

Marsden, William

  The History of Sumatra, Oxford University Press, Kuala
  Lumpur 1966.

Marx, Karl and Engels, F.

  On Colonialism, Foreign Publishing House, Moscow
  n.d.

Money, J. W. B.

  Java, Volumes 1 and 2, Hurst and Blackett, London
  1861.

Moon, P. T.

  Imperialism and World Politics, Macmillan, New York
  1928.

Macdonald, Capt. D.

  A Narrative of the Early Life and Services, Weymouth,
  London [1830].

Moor, J. H.

  Notices of the Indian Archipelago and Adjacent Countries,
  Frank Cass, London 1968. First edition, 1837.

Mukherjee, Ramkrishna

  The Rise and Fall of the East India Company, Deutscher
  Verlag der Wissenschaften, Berlin 1958.

Munshi, Abdullah bin Abdul Kadir

Hikayat Abdullah, R. A. Datoek Besar and R. Roelvink (eds.), Djambatan, Djakarta 1953.

Nadel, G. H. and Curtis, P. (eds.)

Imperialism and Colonialism, Macmillan, New York 1964.

Nahuijs, Lt-Colonel

Brieven over Bencoolen, Padang, het Rijk van Menangk-abau, Rhiauw, Sincapoera en Poelo Pinang, Hollingerus Pijpers, Breda MDCCCXXVI.

Owen, Robert

A New View of Society and Other Writings, Everyman's Library, London 1963.

Patterson, Orlando

The Sociology of Slavery, MacGibbon and Kee, London 1967.

Phillips, C. H. (ed.)

Handbook of Oriental History, Royal Historical Society, London 1951.

Pierson, N. G.

Koloniale Politiek, van Kempen, Amsterdam 1877.

Raffles, Thomas

Letters during a Tour through Some Parts of France, Savoy, Switzerland, Germany, and the Netherlands in the Summer of 1817 (publisher unknown), Liverpool 1817.

Raffles, T. S.

Discourse delivered at a meeting of the Society on the 23rd

April 1813, Transaction of the Batavian Society of Arts and Sciences, Vol. VII, Batavia 1814.

The History of Java, Vols. 1 and 2, reprint of 1817 edition, Oxford University Press, London and Kuala Lumpur 1965.

Raffles, Sophia

Memoir of the Life and Public Services of Sir Thomas Stamford Raffles, Volumes I and II, John Duncan, London 1835.

Memoir of the Life and Public Services of Sir Thomas Stamford Raffles, John Murray, London 1830.

Schrieke, B.

Indonesian Sociological Studies, Part I, van Hoeve, The Hague 1955.

Shepherd, W. R.

"The Expansion of Europe", *Political Science Quarterly*, Vol. 34, 1919, pp. 43-60, 210-25, 392-412.

Smith, Adam

The Wealth of Nations, E. Cannon (ed.), Vol. 2, Methuen, London 1961.

Stibbe, D. G. (ed.)

"T. S. Raffles" in *Encyclopaedic van Nederlandsch-Indie*, Vol. 3, Martinus Nijhoff, The Hague and Brill, Leiden 1919, pp. 532-3.

Strausz-Hupe, R. and Hazard, H. W. (eds.)

The Idea of Colonialism, Atlantic Books, London 1958.

Synder, L. S. (ed.)

The Imperial Reader, Van Nostrand, New York 1962.

Temminck, M.

"Temminck's General View of the Dutch Possession in the Indian Archipelago", *The Journal of the Indian Archipelago and Eastern Asia*, Singapore 1847, pp. 129-49, 183-222.

University of Singapore Library

Raffles Collection, Vol. IV. Microfilms.

Veth, P. J.

Borneo's Wester-Afdeeling, Volumes 1 and 2, Noman en Zoon, Zaltbommel 1854, 1856.

Java, Vol. 2, Bohn, Haarlem 1898.

Winch, D

James Mill—Selected Economic Writings, Oliver and Boyd, London 1966.

Wright, H. R.C.

East-Indian Economic Problems of the Age of Cornwallis and Raffles, Luzac, London 1961.

"The Freedom of Labour under Raffles' Administration in Java (1811-1816)", *JMBRAS*, Vol. XXVI, Pt 1, 1953.

Wright, M. M. (ed.)

The New Imperialism, Heath, Boston 1961.

Wurtzburg, C. E.

"Raffles and the Massacre of Palembang", *JMBRAS*, Vol. XXII, Pt 1,1949.

Raffles of the Eastern Isles, Hodder and Stoughton, London 1954.

[Author unknown]

"De Moord der Hollanders in 1811", *TNI*, Vol. 8, No. 3, 1846.